More on C# in Front Office

- Advanced C# in Practice

Xing ZHOU

This book is NOT the 2nd edition of the previous book *C# in Front Office* (ISBN: 144215358X). Instead, it covers many new topics and has lots of additional information. All contents in this book are chosen based on feedbacks, comments and questions from readers of the previous book.

Some of the code samples in this book can be downloaded from the following address: http://book.greenwich2greenwich.com.

As always, your comments, questions and feedback are more than welcomed. My email address is: geenwich2greenwich@gmail.com.

Thanks for your interest in my book.

Table of Contents

1 MORE ON EXCEL UDF   **9**

1.1 PROCESS VECTOR / MATRIX...**10**
1.1.1   VECTOR / MATRIX AS INPUT   10
1.1.2   VECTOR / MATRIX AS OUTPUT   12
1.1.3   CONVERT TO A COLLECTION OF KEY-VALUE PAIRS   13
1.2 PROCESS DATE...**14**
1.2.1   OVERVIEW   14
1.2.2   A PRACTICAL EXAMPLE – *DATEADD()*   16
1.2.3   OTHER FEATURES (BUSINESS CALENDAR ETC)   21
1.3 HIDE "UNWANTED" FUNCTIONS IN EXCEL FUNCTION WIZARD......**22**
1.3.1   A SIMPLE SOLUTION   24
1.3.2   A BETTER SOLUTION   26
1.4 DEVELOP C# UDF WITHOUT VISUAL STUDIO **28**

2 MORE ON SCRIPTING   **31**

2.1 DEBUGGING DYNAMIC SCRIPT..**31**
2.1.1   INTRODUCTION   31
2.1.1. SCRIPT DEBUGGING IN C++   31
2.1.2. SCRIPT DEBUGGING IN C#   34
2.1.3. MYUTIL.STARTDEBUG()   40
2.1.4. REVISED SCRIPT ENGINE IMPLEMENTATION   42
2.2 MULTIPLE SCRIPT SOURCE FILES...**45**

3 MORE ON C# / C++ INTEGRATION   **47**

3.1 DEBUG C#/C++ HYBRID APPLICATIONS **47**

4   MORE ON THREADING   **51**

4.1   PROTECT CRITICAL RESOURCE **52**
4.1.1   RACE CONDITION   52
4.1.2   USING *LOCK* STATEMENT   55
4.1.3   THE *INTERLOCKED* CLASS   56
4.1.4   THE *MONITOR* CLASS   57
4.1.5   THREAD RE-ENTRY   60
4.1.6   READER LOCK AND WRITER LOCK   61
4.2   AVOID DEADLOCK **67**
4.3   LAZY CACHING AND DOUBLE-CHECKING **70**
4.4   ELIMINATE UNNECESSARY LOCKING – A PRACTICAL EXAMPLE **75**
4.5   DOUBLE-BUFFER PATTERN - A PRACTICAL EXAMPLE **78**
4.6   THREAD SYNCHRONIZATION **83**
4.6.1   SHARE DATA   85
4.6.2   SYNCHRONIZE EXECUTION FLOW   86
4.7   MONTE CARLO **95**
4.8   INTER-PROCESS SYNCHRONIZATION **98**
4.8.1   SYNCHRONIZE EXECUTION FLOW   98
4.8.2   SHARE DATA   101
4.9   DEBUG A MULTITHREADED APPLICATION **103**

5   DEVELOP CLIENT APPLICATIONS   **107**

5.1   OVERVIEW AND DESIGN GUIDELINE **107**
5.2   C# SOLUTION STRUCTURE **109**
5.3   C# APPLICATION AS CLIENT APPLICATION **113**
5.4   VB APPLICATION AS CLIENT APPLICATION **116**
5.5   EXCEL AS CLIENT APPLICATION **120**
5.6   WEB CLIENT **125**

6   DEBUGGING TIPS   **131**

6.1   DISPLAY CUSTOM DEBUG INFORMATION **131**

2.1.5.   METHOD 1 – TOSTRING()   133
2.1.6.   METHOD 2 – DEBUGGERDISPLAY ATTRIBUTE   134
2.1.7.   METHOD 3 – AUTOEXP.CS   139

INDEX OF EXAMPLES   **141**

INDEX OF FIGURES   **143**

1 More on Excel UDF

In the previous book, *C# in Front Office*, we have discussed how to develop Excel user defined functions (UDFs) using C#. It is based on COM automation technology which is different from the traditional C++ based approach. Compared with the traditional C++ based approach, the C# based approach is clearly much simpler, more flexible and more intuitive. What is also important is that the C# based approach requires little to none extra learning curve beyond "regular" C# development skills. This means that any C# developer who can develop and debug regular C# programs can readily develop and debug C# based Excel UDFs. This feature can easily be translated to higher productivity in practice.

In this chapter, we will discuss some additional details and topics that are related to UDF development but have not been covered in the previous book. These contents are chosen based on readers' feedback, comments and questions that have been received since publish of the previous book.

In order to keep this book concise and avoid unnecessary duplication, we will not discuss basic techniques of developing a UDF library using C# here. It is assumed that readers have already gained some practical working knowledge of developing Excel UDF libraries using C#. Otherwise, it is strongly suggested that readers should acquire such knowledge before continuing on this chapter. This can be done by either reading the 1st chapter of the previous book or taking some relevant training.

1.1   Process Vector / Matrix

1.1.1   Vector / Matrix as Input

Vectors and matrices are basic but very important mathematic data types. They are widely used in front office analytic libraries. As such, it is a natural requirement to process these two data types in UDFs. In this section, we will discuss some practical details and tricks about processing vectors and matrices in C# based UDFs.

On an Excel worksheet, a single-row or a single-column range is a natural representation of a vector; and a multi-row-multi-column range is a natural representation of a matrix. Thus it is intuitive to use Excel's built-in *Range*[1] class as the parameter data type in a UDF to represent vector and/or matrix inputs. In fact, the *Range* class has all the usual properties that we will normally expect from a vector or a matrix class. These include *Rows*, *Columns* and so on. It also has a *Cells* iteration interface for looping through all its cells within this *Range* object. All these give us a clearly defined simple interface to deal with a *Range* object. Therefore, processing vectors/matrices as inputs is very simple and intuitive in C#.

However it is important to note how we should retrieve a numeric value from an individual cell using C#. For performance reason, we should use direct type cast instead of parsing the cell contents as text string first. This is because even though the *Value2* property is declared as *object* type and has a default *ToString()* method, it is

---

[1]   This class is defined in the Excel Object library. It is one of the most important classes when developing Excel related application in both C# and other similar programming languages such as VBA.

actually a *double* if the cell contains a number. Because it is a *double*, we can safely use direct type cast.

This means that we should NOT do something like the following:

```
double value = Double.Parse(cell.Value2.ToString());
```

Instead, we shall use:

```
double value = (double)(cell.Value2);
```

In reality, there will be a noticeable performance difference between these two approaches if we have to process large number of cells.

The following is a very simple example which shows how to handle vectors and/or matrices as inputs. And, in particular, it demonstrates how to retrieve numeric values using the direct type cast as we have just discussed. As the code uses the *Cells* iteration interface, it works for both single-row/column and multi-row/column inputs (i.e. both a vector and a matrix).

Please note that the *ExcelUDFBase* class has been fully discussed in the previous book *C# in Front Office*. It contains all the necessary infrastructural functions to make the class usable as a UDF class. A copy of its source code can be freely downloaded from that book's website[2].

```
[ComVisible(true)
[ClassInterface(ClassInterfaceType.AutoDual)]
```

---

[2]   http://book.greenwich2greenwich.com

```
[Guid("F2719620-DD15-4e83-9E77-EFD27CF89EDE")]
public class VectorAndMatrixSample : ExcelUDFBase
{
  public object MySum(MsExcel.Range Input)
  {
    try
    {
      double sum = 0;
      foreach (MsExcel.Range cell in Input)
      {
        sum += (double)(cell.Value2);
      }
      return sum;
    }
    catch (Exception err_)
    {
      return err_.ToString();
    }
  }
}
```

Example 1 Process Vectors and Matrices

1.1.2   Vector / Matrix as Output

To generate a vector or a matrix as a UDF's output is the same thing as returning an *object* array. Developing an array function has been discussed in section 1.8 of the previous book *C# in Front Office*. Thus we will not repeat in details here. In a nutshell, an array function is a regular function that returns an *object*[,] in a C# implementation. If we enter such formula as an array function in an Excel cell (i.e. by pressing *<ctrl>* + *<shift>* + *<enter>*), the output will look like a vector or a matrix on an Excel spreadsheet depending on the dimensions of return data. The previous book has also discussed the technique to ensure the output range has the same dimension as that of the returning vector or matrix. It is very useful in practice not only to beautify the output (e.g. blanketing out additional cells instead of displaying *N/A* when the given Excel range is bigger than the result vector/matrix) but also to avoid potential misleading situation (e.g. missing output data when the given range is smaller than the result vector/matrix).

1.1.3 Convert to a Collection of Key-Value Pairs

Quite often, we need a collection of key-value pairs. A collection of key-value pairs is often used to represent a set of parameters where keys are parameter names and values are parameter values.

On an Excel spreadsheet, we usually use a 2-row or a 2-column range as such inputs. One row (or column) contains parameter names (i.e. the keys) and the other contains corresponding parameter values (i.e. the values). The follow figure shows a pseudo example.

Alpha	Beta	Gama	Delta
1.0	0.5	2.3	4.5

As we can imagine, converting such a range input to a collection of key-value pairs in C# is pretty easy. For practical convenience, we may need a utility function that can automatically detect the shape of an input range (i.e. whether it's 2-row or 2-column). This can help us to extract parameter names and values in a smart way. As the *Range* object gives us a *Rows* and a *Columns* attribute both of which have a *Count* attribute, this auto-detection task is quite easy unless an input happens to be a 2x2 range. If the input is indeed a 2x2 range, we usually have to have a predefined rule, i.e. whether an input will be treated as row significant or column significant in such scenario. Alternatively, if we wish, we may implement a smart strategy. For example we can try to automatically detect which row (or column) contains recognizable parameter names and thus make decision based on this.

A side note on this topic is that it is usually a good idea to convert parameter names to predefined enums in order to detect input errors earlier. It can also help make further processing easier and cleaner. Converting a string to an enum has been discussed in section 7.8 of the previous book *C# in Front Office*.

1.2   Process Date

1.2.1 Overview

In a front office environment, almost all spreadsheets will need to process dates in one way or another. Dates are unquestionably one of the most fundamental and most important data types in a front office application. Therefore handling dates is an important aspect of developing UDFs.

In practice, date expression is very versatile. Sometime it can be hard date value in various formats (e.g. 2010/01/01, Jan 1, 2010 and so on). Sometimes it can be a relative offset (e.g. +7 stands for 7 days after today, or 3M stands for 3 months after today). Sometimes, it can be expressed in market conventions (e.g. 1imm stands for the first so-called IMM date).

C# has a built-in *DateTime* type which provides many basic date and time operations out of box, such as date parsing and so on. What is especially worthy mentioning is that C# has built-in locale support. This feature is somewhat not well utilized in practice. But as trading goes globally and more financial institutions push for synergy among global technology platforms, this feature may become more and more useful. For example, 04/01/2001 means April 1st, 2010 in New York but means January 4th, 2010 in London. Therefore in order to correctly parse this string, we need locale information. Incorrect interpreting of dates may cost dearly to the business. To handle all possible locales using custom code is very tedious and error prone. Fortunately, C# provides us with this capability for free.

Still, C# misses many things that we will need for developing front office applications. These are primarily financial industry specific conventions such as business calendars and so on. Usually we have to write some custom code ourselves if we cannot find a suitable third party package from a trusted software vendor.

In addition, front office users are typically very demanding on user friendliness. They may require functions to be capable of processing various formatted inputs using simple interfaces. This means we may have to combine various basic blocks in order to provide users with a unified and flexible interface.

This section will give a sample date adding function. Some of the techniques presented can be readily reused in other similar real life functions.

1.2.2 A Practical Example – *DateAdd()*

Our sample UDF has the following syntax:

MyDateAdd(*BaseDate, IntervalExpression, Locale*)

Where:

- ➤ *BaseDate*: It supports various hard date formats. If omitted, default to Today.
- ➤ *IntervalExpression*: A numeric value or a valid text string. A valid text string can contain a combination of *y, m* and *d* to indicate year, month and days respectively.
- ➤ *Locale*: If presented, using the given locale to interpret the *BaseDate*. The default value is current locale.

Let's assume that today is 2009/09/27. The following table shows some sample outputs with a default locale set to US.

Function Parameter			Result
Base Date	Interval	Locale	
	1		2009/09/28
	1D		2009/09/28
	1Y3d		2010/09/30
	-3M		2009/06/27
9/30/2009	1		2009/10/01
3/4/2009	1		2009/03/05
3/4/2009	1	en-GB	2009/04/04

The first five examples are self-explanatory. They show flexibility of parameter formats which more or less are what front office users will typically want in real life.

The last two examples demonstrate support of globalization. If no locale is specified (as the 6th example shows), a date string will be interpreted using the computer's default setting (in this case, US). Otherwise, it will be interpreted using the specified locale. What may be even more amazing is the fact that this code can also support non-English input such as Chinese without any modification. It works even if the developer does not understand Chinese at all! A sample output involving Chinese character inputs is given below:

Function Parameter			Result
BaseDate	Interval	Culture	
2009年3月4日	1	zh-CN	2009/03/05

Before we present the source code, we also need to point out some technical details. For example, from a user's perspective, if cell *A1* is an empty cell, the following two calls are the same:

=MyDateAdd(A1, 1,)
=MyDate(,1)

But technically they are different because the former formula points to a valid cell which contains a valid value (which happens to be an empty value). The latter formula simply omits the 1st input. We need to handle this technical difference.

Another example is the difference between a hard input value and a cell reference in the formula. As long as the input value is the same as the contents of the referenced cell, these two cases should yield the same result. So example, if cell *B1* contains a value of 1, the following two calls should be the same:

=MyDateAdd(A1, 1,)
=MyDate(A1,B1)

But again technically they are different. The former formula contains an input value but the latter contains a reference to another cell. Conceptually it is similar to the case in C++ where one contains a value and the other contains a pointer which points to a same value. Depending on the underlying technology that is used to develop UDFs, special handling may be required. The sample code that is shown below can correctly handle both cases.

Some techniques used in the source code, e.g. optional parameters, choice of parameter type declaration (e.g. using *object* instead of a more specific type such as *DateTime* etc), function return (*object* instead of a more intuitive *DateTime*) etc have been discussed in the previous book *C# in Front Office*. In order to keep this book concise, we will not explain them in details here.

```
public object MyDateAdd(
        [Optional, DefaultParameterValue(null)] Object BaseDate
    , Object IntervalExpression
    , [Optional, DefaultParameterValue(null)] String Locale
    )
{
  // Please note there is a testing sheet for this sample
  // The testing sheet can be downloaded from the book's
  // web site: http://book.greenwich2greenwich.com
  try
  {
    // First, we need to determine the base date.
```

```csharp
DateTime baseDate = DateTime.Today;
if (null != BaseDate)
{
  CultureInfo culture = (null == Locale || 0 == Locale.Length)
        ? CultureInfo.CurrentCulture
        : new CultureInfo(Locale)
        ;
  if (BaseDate is MsExcel.Range)
  {
    String value = ((MsExcel.Range)BaseDate).Text.ToString();
    if (value.Length > 0)
    {
      baseDate = DateTime.Parse(value, culture);
    }
  }
  else if(BaseDate is String)
  {
    baseDate = DateTime.Parse(((String)BaseDate), culture);
  }
  else
  {
    baseDate = (DateTime)BaseDate;
  }
}
// next, we need to process the IntervalExpression
object interval = (IntervalExpression is MsExcel.Range)
        ? ((MsExcel.Range)IntervalExpression).Value2
        : IntervalExpression
        ;

if (interval is double)
{
```

```
    return baseDate.AddDays((double)interval);
}
else
{
  // if the given value is text
  String text = interval.ToString();
  String pattern =
        @"^-?((\d+)\s*y)?\s*((\d+)\s*m)?\s*((\d+)\s*d)*$";
  Match match = Regex.Match(
        text, pattern, RegexOptions.IgnoreCase);
  Group yearGroup = match.Groups[2];
  Group monthGroup = match.Groups[4];
  Group dayGroup = match.Groups[6];
  if (yearGroup.Success
     || monthGroup.Success
     || dayGroup.Success
    )
  {
    int year = yearGroup.Success
              ? Int32.Parse(yearGroup.Value) : 0;
    int month = monthGroup.Success
              ? Int32.Parse(monthGroup.Value) : 0;
    int day = dayGroup.Success
              ? Int32.Parse(dayGroup.Value) : 0;
    if (text.StartsWith("-"))
    {
      year = -year;
      month = -month;
      day = -day;
    }
    baseDate = baseDate.AddYears(year);
    baseDate = baseDate.AddMonths(month);
```

```
      baseDate = baseDate.AddDays(day);
      return baseDate;
    }
  }
  // OK, give up.
  return "Invalid input?";
  }
  catch (Exception err_)
  {
    return err_.ToString();
  }
}
```

Example 2 MyDateAdd

1.2.3 Other Features (Business Calendar etc)

In practice, we will need to support some financial industry specific features such as business calendars, date counting rules and so on. These are not available by default in C#. But it is relatively easy to implement in C# because C# has already provided us with many basic building blocks.

The exact implementation strategy of these features can vary and may depend on the developer's preference. Meanwhile it can also depend on the C# version we are using. For example, C# version 3.0 and beyond provides us with a powerful extension method feature. Therefore we can implement these additional methods as extension methods on the native *DateTime* type. This approach can make using these additional features very simple and intuitive. In the following figure, we can see all these extension methods, such as *AddBusinessDays(), AddPeriods()* etc will be automatically available via intellisence for a variable of *DateTime* type.

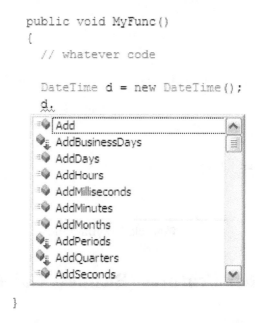

```
public void MyFunc()
{
  // whatever code

  DateTime d = new DateTime();
  d.
```

| Add |
| AddBusinessDays |
| AddDays |
| AddHours |
| AddMilliseconds |
| AddMinutes |
| AddMonths |
| AddPeriods |
| AddQuarters |
| AddSeconds |

```
}
```

Figure 1 Implementing Business Calendar etc Using Extension Method

In C# 2.0 and previous versions where extension method is not available, a typical approach to implement these functions is to use static helper class. Either way, development efforts will usually be similar regardless of implementation strategy.

1.3 Hide "Unwanted" Functions in Excel Function Wizard

One minor but quite annoying detail of a C# based UDF library is that it has some unwanted functions be displayed in the Excel functions wizard.

Let's assume that we have developed a UDF library. This library only contains one function, *MyTestFunction*. When we try to use this library in Excel function wizard, we will see four additional unwanted functions as shown below:

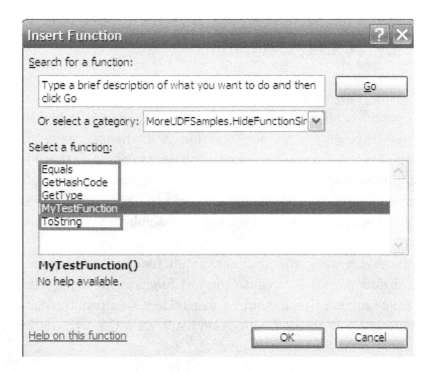

These functions are automatically inherited from the C# root *Object* class. As we have explained in the previous book *C# in Front Office*, any public function in a UDF class may be available as a valid Excel UDF. Therefore these inherited functions, while usually unwanted, will be available to use as valid UDFs and thus be shown in the Excel function wizard.

Even though having these additional functions displayed in the wizard dialogue usually is not a serious problem, it is still somewhat annoying and better to avoid. Fortunately, it is possible to hide those unwanted functions. In this section, we will present two solutions. One solution is relatively simple, but can only hide three of these four unwanted functions. The other is a little bit more complicated, but can hide all these functions.

1.3.1   A Simple Solution

Clearly, the reason that those unwanted functions appear in the function wizard is that they are inherited regular public functions. Even though we cannot override and change these functions' visibility (i.e. from public to private), we can override these functions and then mark them as COM invisible. By doing so, these functions are still public functions and available to C# clients, but invisible to COM clients. As a result, they will be invisible to Excel clients.

However among the four unwanted function, only three can be overridden. This is because the last function, *GetType()*, is a public static function that cannot be overridden. As a result, this approach can only hide three functions and still leave the *GetType()* function visible in Excel function wizard.

A sample code is shown below. Again, the *ExcelUDFBase* class has been fully explained in the previous book.

```
[ComVisible(true)]
[Guid("A0B7A401-1616-426f-ACC7-B61F0F7AA040")]
[ClassInterface(ClassInterfaceType.AutoDual)]
public class HideFunctionSimple : ExcelUDFBase
{
```

```
public object MyTestFunction()
{
  return "OK";
}


[ComVisible(false)]
public override bool Equals(object obj)
{
  return base.Equals(obj);
}


[ComVisible(false)]
public override int GetHashCode()
{
  return base.GetHashCode();
}


[ComVisible(false)]
public override string ToString()
{
  return base.ToString();
}
}
```

Example 3 Hide Unwanted Functions (A Simple Approach)

The following figure shows the result as it is displayed in the Excel function wizard. We can see indeed three of the four unwanted functions are no longer seen.

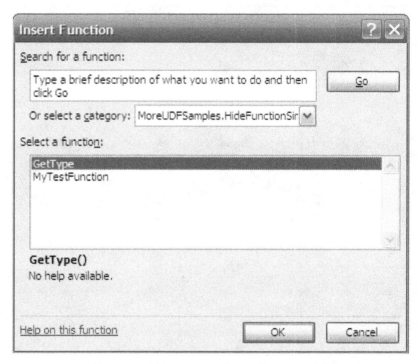

Figure 2 Hide Unwanted UDF functions (1)

1.3.2 A Better Solution

If the previous simple solution is not good enough, we can go for a cleaner solution at the expense of additional complexity.

The basic idea is to define an interface which only contains the list of UDF functions that we want. Then we make our real class implement this interface. By doing this, an Excel client only sees the functions as defined in the interface (i.e. exactly what we want the client to see) regardless of how many public functions that are available in the real concrete class that implements this interface.

A sample program is shown below:

```csharp
using System;
using System.Runtime.InteropServices;

[ComVisible(true)]
public interface MyCleanUDFInterface
{
  object MyTestFunction2();
}

[ComVisible(true)]
[ClassInterface(ClassInterfaceType.None)]
[Guid("54962592-BDD7-4060-8742-B26A6092C904")]
public class HideUnwantedFunctions2
    : ExcelUDFBase, MyCleanUDFInterface
{
  public object MyTestFunction2()
  {
    return "OK";
  }
}
```

Example 4 Hide Unwanted Functions (A Better Approach)

The code is self-explanatory. One important detail that we need to pay attention to here is how we mark our new class. Instead of the usual *ClassInterfaceType.AutoDual* attribute, we now need to use the *ClassInterfaceType.None* attribute. The difference between these two attributes is fully documented in MSDN. Therefore we are not going to discuss here.

With this implementation, we can see only the UDF function we want in Excel function wizard (as shown in the figure below). The result is impressive. However we must pay the cost of defining an interface and keeping this interface synchronized with our real class implementation.

Figure 3 Hide Unwanted UDF functions (2)

1.4   Develop C# UDF without Visual Studio

Typically we will need Visual Studio in order to develop C# libraries including UDF libraries. Usually this is not an issue in a development environment, but it may be an issue in a production environment. This is because many financial institutions' IT and internal control policies forbid installation of development tools in a production environment. We know that Excel UDF development is somewhat special because it is often done in a production environment. Many business users, such as traders, frequently write UDFs by themselves on the trading floor.

Writing UDFs in a production environment using VBA is usually not a problem because VBA development environment comes with Excel installation. It is definitely a problem if we use C++ because writing UDF using C++ will require a C++ development environment. It may be a problem if we use C# because usually we will need Visual Studio to develop a C# library. But it is possible to do so without Visual Studio.

In fact, the solution of developing C# libraries without Visual Studio has already been presented in the previous book *C# in Front Office*. It is in the chapter 3 *Scripting*. In that chapter, we have described how to implement a script engine to compile and execute a C# script. A C# based script is essentially a C# program. If we can compile and build any C# script in runtime without the need of Visual Studio, we can compile and build C# based UDF libraries too. If we take this approach, what we need to do is to have an embedded script editor and corresponding compilation result window into Excel or any other in-house custom built application for users to develop UDFs. Both techniques have already been discussed fully in the previous book. They are able to offer reasonably high quality experience to users.

Clearly, this is already much better than a C++ approach because without a development environment (compiler, linker and all related libraries etc), it is almost impossible to build any C++ library. As such it is certainly a show-stop if users want to develop C++ based UDFs in a production environment without any development tool.

However, compared with the VBA approach, the C# approach still misses one important capability without Visual Studio. That is the debugging capability. It is possible to develop and compile C# library without Visual Studio in a very user friendly way. But it is usually impossible to debug the code without a debugger which is typically the Visual Studio itself. The next chapter is dedicated to dynamic script debugging. The technique presented there also applies to UDF library debugging. However, if Visual Studio is not allowed to be installed but we still want to have the debugging capability, we will have to find an alternative debugger or develop a custom debugging tool. Both approaches will be quite difficult.

2 More on Scripting

2.1 Debugging Dynamic Script

2.1.1 Introduction

Chapter 3 of the previous book *C# in Front Office* has introduced a C# based dynamic scripting engine implementation. As it shows, a C# based scripting engine is much simpler and more intuitive to develop than a typical C++ approach is. Meanwhile, a C# approach can offer much more powerful features than a typical C++ implementation can.

However the previous book has left out an important practical matter. That is how to debug a dynamic script. As every technologist can testify, debugging is as important as, if not more important than, writing and compiling code. This sector will discuss how to debug dynamic scripts.

2.1.1. Script Debugging in C++

In order to appreciate the power of C# in dynamic script debugging, we shall understand what we need when debugging a dynamic script and what a C++ implementation fails to offer.

In a typical C++ based script engine implementation, debugging a user script is a very difficult task. In order to debug a user script, a developer usually has to recompile the whole script engine itself in debug mode. Debugging script essentially becomes debugging the script engine. What's more inconvenient and counterintuitive is that we cannot set breakpoints in a user script itself. Instead, we have to set breakpoint in the script parsing or execution code which is part of the script engine itself. In practice, many script developers are not involved in scripting engine development. Thus they are unlikely familiar with script engine implementation. As a result, they have to take some additional script engine specific training in order to get themselves familiar with script engine implementation. As we know, a C++ based scripting engine can be quite complicated. Therefore it can be quite a learning curve for a script developer to be able to debug dynamic scripts efficiently.

In order to understand a script engine implementation, developers will typical need to have some understanding of how script parsing and execution works. This is certainly not rocket science, but is still a bit involved.

Expressions are basic building blocks of a script. Therefore, let's take expression parsing and execution as an example.

Expression parsing is usually done by representing this expression as a tree structure. For example, the following simple express can be represented by a tree structure shown below.

A + B * C

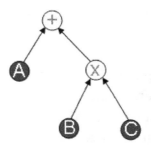

In such an expression tree structure, all leafs contain actual values and all nodes contain operators. When this tree is evaluated (i.e. the original expression is to be executed), a leaf-to-node deepest first search is carried out. So for example, in this given tree above, the script engine will take two leafs B and C then apply the operator *multiple* to them. This will produce the result of B * C which forms a new leaf. This new leaf will then be combined with leaf A before applying the operator *plus* in order to get the final result.

As we can see and imagine, both the logic to build a tree structure from a given expression and the logic to evaluate such a tree can be very generic and abstract. For example, tree evaluation logic may be just some recursive code that is largely based on a standard tree deepest first search algorithm. Due to the nature of recursive algorithm, it is quite difficult to determine which part of the tree is currently being evaluated during a debug session. As a matter of practical reality, many technologists will choose to write down the tree structure on a piece of paper and trace the execution by hand while debugging a script in order to determine which part of the expression tree is currently being evaluated. Even so, quite often, people will still get lost pretty quickly if the expression is a bit complicated. Many people may turn to more primitive approach, e.g. inserting lots of print statements, when debugging user scripts. Clearly this is a very tedious approach because we need to recompile the whole script engine whenever we have inserted or removed a print statement.

We also need to realize that a typical script will contain lots of expressions. All these expressions will be processed by the same code within the script engine. This means that even if we may just be interested in one particular expression among them, we may have to be quite patiently watching the script engine to process all the expressions using the same logic and carefully determine whether the expression that we are interested is currently being processed. When that expression is being processed, we also need to figure out which part of the expression is being processed currently. Obviously, this will by no means be a pleasant debugging experience.

It is fair to say debugging a user script in a typical C++ based script engine implementation is very frustrating which can be translated to low productivity in real life.

2.1.2. Script Debugging in C#

What we are going to show in this section may seem to be a too good to be true story. However, script debugging in a C# based script engine implementation is indeed extremely simple and intuitive. Again, any technologist with basic C# skill can debug a user script easily without much additional learning curve.

Firstly, we don't need to recompile the script engine in debug mode in order to debug a user script. We can debug a user script within an engine which was built in release mode. This means we no longer need to switch between two different builds of a script engine in order to debug our script. This will make it possible to debug a script on a user's production environment using a release version script engine. Being able to debug user scripts using a release built script engine also implies that developers do not need to understand the internal logic within the script engine. This clearly is a productivity gain in practice.

Secondly, we can set breakpoints in a user script itself directly. This is very interesting and makes debugging a script same as debugging a regular C# program. In fact, this feature may be the most attractive feature in a C# based script engine implementation. As we can easily see, this is a huge productivity gain.

Finally, all these desirable features come for free in a C# based script engine implementation. This means great product quality assurance because of less custom code.

For demonstration purpose, let's use the following user script as a sample input.

```csharp
using System;
public class MyScript
{
  public void Run()
  {
    Console.WriteLine("OK");
  }
}
```

To debug this script, all we need to do is to insert some function calls as following in an appropriate location:

```
using System;
using System.Diagnostics;

public class MyScript
{
  public void Run()
  {
    Debugger.Launch();
    Debugger.Break();
    Console.WriteLine("OK");
  }
}
```

Example 5 Debug-able Dynamic Script

The *Debugger.Launch*() statement will launch the Visual Studio debugger and attach it to the current process.

The *Debugger.Break*() statement will force the execution to break at the specific location.

When we execute this script as usual[3], we will see the following dialogue to be displayed:

---

[3]   We need to modify our script engine a little bit to compile this script in debug mode. This is very easy and will be discussed later.

If you already have an instance of Visual Studio running, the dialogue will also give you a choice to use one of these existing instances of Visual Studio.

If we make our choice of Visual Studio and then click the *YES* button, an instance of Visual Studio will be launched. If the script engine itself was built in release mode, an information dialogue which is similar to the following will pop up. Otherwise if the script engine was built in debug mode, we will skip this dialogue.

The above dialogue basically says the script engine itself was built in release mode. Because of this, we will be unable to debug the script engine itself. However Visual Studio will still allow us to debug other debuggable code such as the user scripts. If the script engine itself was built in debug mode, we will not see this dialogue because we will be able to debug the script engine itself.

If we click away this information dialogue, we will see our user script is automatically loaded into Visual Studio and code execution breaks at the *Debugger.Launch()* statement. This is shown in the following figure.

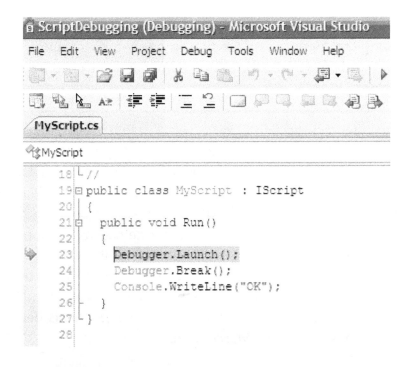

At this point, we can debug this user script as if it is a regular C# program. This means we can step over, step into and run the code. We can also inspect the value of any variables as we can do when debugging a regular C# program.

It is important to note that because the debugger (i.e. Visual Studio in this case) fully recognizes the script source code, we can directly set breakpoints in the script and inspect any variable as we usually do. For example, if we set a breakpoint at line 25 in the above figure and click run, the code will break at line 25. As mentioned before this is a significant improvement over script debugging in a typical C++ based engine implementation. And we get this wonderful feature for free without any additional development efforts.

We also note that if the script engine was built in debug mode, we can actually continue debugging into the script engine itself after exiting the user script if we have a need to do so. But if we don't want to debug the script engine itself, we don't need a debug built engine.

The difference occurs after we have stepped over the last script statement, i.e. the closing bracket at line 26. If the script engine was built in release mode, Visual Studio will give us a choice whether to continue debugging the .NET MISL code which is compiled low level instructions (instead of the original C# source code). If the script engine was built in debug mode, the debugging session will step back into the script engine code. This means, if the script engine has the following code (as the example given in the previous book, *C# in Front Office*), the current statement-being-debugged will be the closing bracket after the *((IScript)object).Run()*. This is because this statement executes the *MyScript::Run()* method.

```
if (null != classname)
{
  object obj =
result.CompiledAssembly.CreateInstance(classname);
  ((IScript)obj).Run()
}
```

2.1.3. MyUtil.StartDebug()

In practice, it is often better to wrap the debug enabling code into a utility method as shown below. It can also make our code a little bit more robust in case multiple *Debugger.Lanuch()* statements are inserted into the user script.

```
using System;
using System.Diagnostics;
public class MyScriptUtil
{
    public static void StartDebug()
    {
      if (!Debugger.IsAttached)
      {
        Debugger.Launch();
      }
      Debugger.Break();
    }
}
```

Example 6 MyScriptUtil.StartDebug()

Using the above utility method, we can simplify the previous sample script to the following:

```
using System;
public class MyScript
{
  public void Run()
  {
    MyUtil.StartDebug();
    Console.WriteLine("OK");
  }
}
```

Example 7 A Debuggable User Script

2.1.4. Revised Script Engine Implementation

As we have shown, from the user perspective, inserting a statement of *MyUtil.StartDebug()* is all it takes to debug a user script. However this has an implicit assumption that the user script was compiled in debug mode. Otherwise we will be unable to debug user script at the source code level. (We will still be able to debug its MISL code. But this is not what we want.)

The script engine implementation example we gave in the previous book, *C# in Front Office,* will compile all user scripts in release mode. Therefore the question is how to compile user scripts in debug mode? Fortunately, the solution is very simple and intuitive. All we need is to specify the following flags in the compiler options when compiling user scripts.

```
option.IncludeDebugInformation = true;
option.GenerateInMemory = false;
// this is required as we say not to generate in memory
option.OutputAssembly = "MyScript.dll";
```

Example 8 Compile Script in Debug Mode

These are self-explanatory. If we want to debug a script, we need to include debugging information during compilation. We also need to store such information somewhere so that a debugger (i.e. Visual Studio) can find them during a debug session later on. It is important to point out that all we need is that the assembly generated from the user script contains debugging information, not the script engine itself. This is why whether the script engine was built in debug mode is irrelevant to script debugging.

The following sample code is very similar to the sample complier shown in the book *C# in Front Office*[4]. The only difference is that this sample script engine will compile script in debug mode.

```csharp
using System;
using System.CodeDom;
using System.CodeDom.Compiler;
using System.Reflection;
using Microsoft.CSharp;


public class Program
{
  static void Main()
  {
    ScriptDebuggingSample script = new ScriptDebuggingSample();
    script.Example1();
  }
}

public class ScriptDebuggingSample
{
  public void Example1()
  {
    CSharpCodeProvider provider = new CSharpCodeProvider();
    CompilerParameters option = GetCompilerOption();
    CompilerResults result = provider.CompileAssemblyFromFile(
            option, "MyScript.cs");
    object instance = result.CompiledAssembly.CreateInstance(
            "MyScript");
    MethodInfo method = instance.GetType().GetMethod("Run");
    method.Invoke(instance, null);
```

---

[4]   Example 15 on page 76 of *C# in Front Office*.

```
    }

  private static CompilerParameters GetCompilerOption()
  {
    CompilerParameters option = new CompilerParameters();
    option.GenerateInMemory = false;
    option.IncludeDebugInformation = true;
    option.OutputAssembly = "MyScript.dll";
    return option;
  }

}
```

Example 9 Dynamic Script Driver

Certainly we don't want to compile scripts in debug mode if we are not going to debug. Therefore we want our engine a little bit smarter to decide whether it shall compile user script in debug mode or in release mode. There are several different ways to achieve this goal. One is to scan the script source, if it contains uncommented out *MyUtil.StartDebug()*, we will compile the script in debug mode, otherwise we compile it in release mode. As we have seen, the only difference is to specify different *CompilerParameters*. Therefore the implementation will be very simple.

In practice, there is one subtle implication we must consider. When we execute an assembly, the assembly will be loaded to memory and thus cannot be overwritten. This means that after we have compiled an assembly in debug mode (i.e. have generated a physical DLL file) and then have executed it, we cannot recompile in again. If we attempted to do so, we will get an error message saying the output file is currently locked by another process. There are several different approaches to solve this issue. An obvious solution is to specify different output file name during each compilation. This method will certainly work, but may leave us with some clean-up work in order to delete all those generated assembly DLL files. Alternatively, we can execute the script in a separate *AppDomain*. This will allow us to unload our assembly by unloading that *AppDomain*. This usually is a very clean solution.

2.2   Multiple Script Source Files

In practice, we often need to have multiple script sources organized in a similar way as a C# project does. For example, we may want to group some common utility functions in a shared script source file which can be referenced by different other scripts. Essentially, this is a question of how to reference other scripts as needed.

We can certainly simulate the project file approach as we see in almost all modern development environments. This approach is to organize multiple source files into one or more projects. We can also use other simpler alternative such as putting special tags in the script sources to indicate such reference relationship. For example, we can use the following directive at the beginning of a user script to indicate this script depends on the *MyUtils* script in the *CommLib* directory.

```
/// REQUIRE: CommonLib/MyUtils
```

Then we can identify all the dependent scripts by scanning source scripts in a recursive mode.

No matter which approach we take, the information we want to extract is a list of scripts that the current script depends on. Now, let's assume that we know the to-be-compiled main script and all the scripts that it depends on, then all we need to do is to supply this list to the *CompileAssembleFromFile()* method during compilation. It is equivalent to supply multiple source files when using C# compiler *cs.exe* in the command line mode.

3 More on C# / C++ Integration

3.1 Debug C#/C++ Hybrid Applications

In many front office environments, it is quite common to see some C++/C# hybrid applications. A typical example is a C# based GUI as a front-end and a C++ based analytic library as a back-end. To some extents, C# based Excel UDF also falls into this category. Such design can bring the best of both languages together. There are several different approaches to integrate C# and C++ components. Chapter 4 of the previous book *C# in Front Office* is dedicated to this topic.

This section is to discuss how to debug a C# / C++ hybrid application. Even though in reality many technologists don't know how to debug a C++/C# hybrid application, debugging such a hybrid application is actually quite easy and straight-forward. It is natively supported by Visual Studio.

In order to master the relevant debugging technique, we must first understand some terminologies. In Microsoft's world, code written in C# is referred as managed code and code written in C++ is referred as unmanaged code. Unmanaged code sometime is also referred as native code.

By default, when we debug an application, Visual Studio will be able to detect which language is used to develop the entry point module. Therefore if we debug a C# application, Visual Studio will be able to automatically set itself to debug managed code. Likewise, if we debug a C++ application, Visual Studio will be able to automatically set itself to debug unmanaged code. All these happen automatically without our notice. But when we debug a hybrid application, there may be a problem. For example, if the front-end of the application, i.e. the entry module, is written in C#, Visual Studio will set itself to debug managed code. Therefore even if we compile the back-end C++ module in debug mode and set breakpoints there, these breakpoints will not be triggered. This is the most commonly seen frustration in debugging a hybrid application. If we understand the reason why code execution won't break in the back-end C++ code, we can easily find the solution. Indeed, the solution is to set Visual Studio to debug both managed and unmanaged code. This can be done by setting a debugger option. In the next several pages, we will discuss how to set this option.

Similar to debug a regular C# application, there are two methods that can be used to debug a C#/C++ hybrid application. One is to start a debug session by launching the project directly inside Visual Studio. The short-cut key is *F5*. The other is to attach Visual Studio to a running process. Either method will work.

For illustration purpose, let's assume that we need to debug a hybrid application with a C# front-end and a C++ back-end. The same technique can also be used to debug a hybrid application with a C++ front-end and a C# back-end.

If we plan to start debugging by directly launching a project inside Visual Studio, this option is in the project properties. Right-clicking mouse on the C# project, select the *Debug* tab and then tick the *Enable Unmanaged Code Debugging* option. That's all we need to do. Then we can start debugging as usual, such as by pressing *F5*. The code will break at any breakpoint set in the C++ source code.

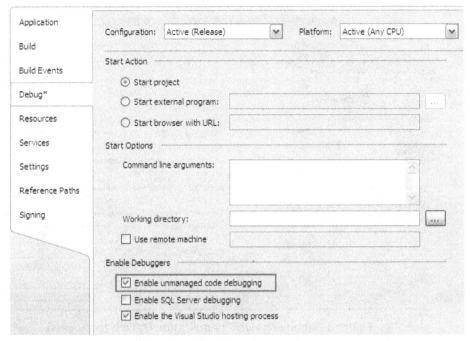

Figure 4 Debugging Hybrid Application (Project Settings)

If we plan to start debugging by attaching an instance of Visual Studio to a running process, the option will appear when we are about to attach to a process. Select from the menu *Tool* and then *Attach to Process*. This will bring a dialogue window like the following figure. If we debug a regular application, we just need to double click on the process. If we need to debug a hybrid application, all we need to do is to select the *Native Code* option as highlighted below before attaching to the target process. After selecting this option, code execution will stop when any C++ breakpoint is hit.

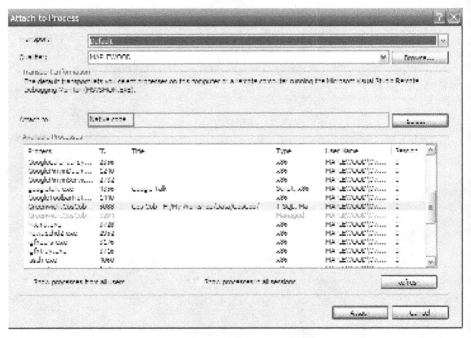

Figure 5 Debugging Hybrid Application (Attach to Process)

BTW, we also need to point out that the same debugging technique can be used in debugging an Excel add-in written in hybrid fashion.

4 More on Threading

It is certainly fair to say that multithread programming is the same between developing a C++ application and a C# application. Both need to solve same problems, avoid same pitfalls and usually use the same techniques to achieve these objectives. However, unlike C++, C# provides many native supports for multithreading development. For example, in C#, thread and various mutex classes are standard native classes. In C++, we usually need to find some third-party libraries for equivalent of these classes. It is easy to see that having a set of standard built-in classes will be of great help in improving product quality and lowing training cost. This is because developers do not need to learn many different things for essentially same functionalities. It also makes it possible for developers to develop advanced skills easier by continuously working on the same set of classes and related technologies.

In reality, there are still many front office technologists who are very skilled in developing analytic libraries but somewhat unfamiliar with or uncomfortable about writing multithreaded applications. Others, even though familiar with multithreading programming, may not be aware of some practical patterns and special techniques that are very unique in developing front office specific application. Some of such techniques may be somewhat different from what they have learned from classic multithread programming in the past. But these special techniques are actually very effective in solving certain types of common issues front office technologists often face.

This chapter will cover both areas. For concise reason, we will keep some basic and self-explanatory contents short and focus more on those relatively complex and, especially, practical patterns and useful techniques.

4.1 Protect Critical Resource

4.1.1 Race Condition

It may be fair to say that the top issue in multithread programming is to make results are deterministic by ensuring critical resources to be accessed only by one thread at a time. In the simplest form, critical resource refers to those shared data that may be accessed by several different threads.

When the result is not deterministic, we have a race condition. To see a simple example of race condition, let's assume we have a data member, *myCounter*, which is to track some counting result. It will be updated by several threads. Each thread will increase *myCounter* by one after having performed some tasks. If within each thread, we simply increase *myCounter* as we usually do in a single threaded manner, e.g. ++*myCounter*, we may end up with incorrect counting. In another word, this implementation may cause a race condition. The root cause of this problem is that even the simplest operator such as ++ is not atomic therefore the overall result may depend on thread execution sequence. If an operator is not atomic, it means that this operator will map to multiple internal low level instructions. When CPU executes code, it executes those low level instructions. For example, a ++ operator may internally map to the following three low-level instructions:

1. Read the current value of *myCounter* from RAM to CPU cache
2. Increase the value in CPU cache by one
3. Write the value in CPU cache back to the RAM

In a single threaded application, there is only one execution thread and all instructions will be executed in sequential manner. Therefore whether an operator is atomic does not really matter. However in a multithread application, whether an operator is atomic turns out to be very important. This is because other threads may jump in at any time when one thread is executing. If an operator is not atomic, we may end up a situation where "part" of the operator is executed and the rest is not. Sometime this may lead to undesirable results, e.g. race conditions.

To see an example of race condition, let's assume there are two threads, *T1* and *T2* both of which are executing the *++MyCounter* statement. The initial value of *myCounter* is 0. We will naturally expect the final value of *myCounter* will be 2 after both *T1* and *T2* have increased it by one. However its value may end up with either 1 or 2, i.e. the result is not deterministic.

To get a final result of 2 is easy. We only need to assume T1 has completed the three low level instructions without being interrupted before T2 completes the three low level instructions.

To get a final result of 1 requires a little bit coincidence. Here is an example. Let's assume *T1* first completed the 1st and 2nd low level instruction. Therefore it first gets the initial value of 0 and then increases it to 1. Please note that, at this moment, the value of 1 is still held in CPU cache and has not been written back to the RAM. Now let's assume *T2* kicks in at this moment and completed all the three low level instructions. Therefore it reads the initial value of 0 (because it has not been updated by *T1* yet), increases it by 1 and writes the value back to RAM. Now it's *T1*'s turn to complete its 3rd low level instruction. As we can imagine, it will write the value of 1 as it holds in the CPU cache back to RAM which will simply overwrite the value written by *T2* earlier. As a result, we will end up with a final result of 1 after both threads have completed their execution.

The following table summarizes the execution sequence as described above.

T1	T2	myCounter Value		
		in RAM	CPU cache (when T1 I executing)	CPU cache (when T2I executing)
		0	-	-
Step 1 - Load RAM to CPU Cache		0	0	-
Step 2 - Increase by 1		0	1	-
	Step 1 - Load RAM to CPU Cache	0		0
	Step 2 - Increase by 1	0		1
	Step 3 - Write back to RAM	1		1
Step 3 - Write back to RAM		1	1	

Figure 6 Race Condition

The nature of multithreading determines that there is no way we can predict the exact executing sequence of different threads. A thread may be suspended at any point. Therefore in the example we just gave, the result is not deterministic. This also means that the result is non-reproducible. In practice, non-reproducible results are very bad, even worse than reproducible incorrect results. This is because the former case is much more difficult than the latter to troubleshoot and fix.

To eliminate race condition is undoubtedly the number one priority in multithreading programming. Fortunately, solution is pretty simple. That is to make operations on shared data atomic. To put it in another way, this is equivalent to allow only one thread to access shared data (i.e. critical resource) at a time. In the previous example, if we can ensure that all the three low level instructions will be executed together by one thread without being interrupted, we will be certain that the final result of *MyCounter* will be 2.

4.1.2 Using *lock* statement

In order to protect critical resource, we will need a lock. Each piece of critical resource should be associated with one dedicated lock. Any thread that wishes to manipulate a piece of critical resource must acquire the corresponding lock first. A lock can only be owned by one thread at a time.

In C#, the simplest way to implement the above logic is to use the *lock* statement. The following sample code is a thread-safe version of the example that we just gave in the previous section. The code is self-explanatory. It uses the *lock* statement to guard *myCounter's* incremental operation.

```
int myCounter = 0;
object myCounterLock = new object();

void MyThreadLogic()
{
  // ... whatever other logic ...
  lock (myCounterLock)
  {
    ++myCounter;
  }
  // ... whatever other logic ...
}
```

Example 10 Lock Statement

A lock is an object. In fact, it can be an instance of any object. As such, we can simply create a dummy object *myCounterLock* to be used for this purpose. We can also use any other object instance that exists in the code such as *this* or even the critical resource itself. However, usually it is a good idea to avoid using the critical resource itself or, especially, *this* as the lock. This is to eliminate unnecessary blocking of other harmless threads from executing unrelated code. This is because if we have locked *this* pointer, we essentially have locked the whole object itself. This means no other thread can access *this* pointer even if that thread is completely irrelevant to the critical resource we aim to protect. A minor side issue is that a program may contain multiple pieces of independent critical resources. If we use *this* as the lock object for all these critical resources, we will create unnecessary dependencies.

4.1.3 The *Interlocked* class

Sometimes, we just want to make some simple operations atomic, such as assignment, increment and decrement. The example we gave in section 4.1 on page 52 is such a case. In these cases, creating a dummy lock object to be used with *lock* statement just to guard a simple operation appears to be somewhat a bit too heavy.

C# provides a short-cut alternative specifically for such cases. It is the *Interlocked* class. This is a very simple class and is well documented in MSDN. Here we just provide an alternative to Example 10 by using the *interlocked* class in order to demonstrate its usage.

```
void MyThreadLogic()
{
```

```
// ... whatever other logic ...
System.Threading.Interlocked.Increment(ref myCounter);
// ... whatever other logic ...
}
```

Example 11 Interlocked class

As we can see from the above example, we can view *Interlocked* class as an operator wrapper. Its sole purpose is to make a simple operator atomic therefore that operator can be used in a thread safe manner.

4.1.4 The *Monitor* class

The *lock* statement which has been described in section 4.1.2 on page 55 turns out to be a shortcut usage of the *Monitor* class. While the *lock* statement is very intuitive and simple to use, it does not provide us with much fine control. Its sole purpose is for a thread to make an attempt to acquire a lock. If that lock is currently owned by another thread, it will cause this thread to wait infinitively until the lock is released and acquired by itself.

In practice, quite often, we need a finer control. For example, if a lock is currently owned by another thread, we may wish to have the opportunity to walk away to do something else and come back for another try later. This is a very practical and effective technique to improve overall program performance if that thread is a long running thread. In order to achieve such finer control, we need the *Monitor* class.

The usage of the *Monitor* class is as intuitive as the *lock* statement. The basic concept is the same, but the *Monitor* class provides more methods for us to have finer control of how we want to handle some specific situations.

Firstly, let's see give an example of how to use the Monitor class to re-implement Example 10:

```
int myCounter = 0;
object myCounterLock = new object();


void MyThreadLogic()
{
  // ... whatever other logic ...
  Monitor.Enter(myCounterLock);
  try
  {
    ++myCounter;
  }
  finally
  {
    try
    {
      Monitor.Exit(myCounterLock);
    }
    catch { }
  }
  // ... whatever other logic ...
}
```

Example 12 Monitor.Enter() / Monitor.Exit()

The code above is self-explanatory. If we compare this example with the previous example, we can see that essentially the *lock* statement is a short-cut of using the *Monitor* class within a try-catch setup.

Before we move further, we must point out that it is important to exit every *Monitor* that the thread has entered. In another word, it is important to make sure the number of times that *Monitor.Enter*() has been called equal to the number of times that *Monitor.Exit*() has been called. Otherwise, we will cause serious thread lock issues and unexpected exceptions. This is the reason we usually must put the *Monitor.Exit*() in the *finally* block.

The *Monitor* class also provides a *TryEnter*() method which allows us to specify a timeout period. If the to-be-acquired lock is locked and still has not successfully acquired by expiry, this thread will skip the attempt and continue executing the next statement. Below is an example to demonstrate how to use the *TryEnter()* method with an expiry setting.

```
int myCounter = 0;
object myCounterLock = new object();

void MyThreadLogic()
{
  // ... whatever other logic ...
  if (Monitor.TryEnter(myCounterLock, 1000))
  {
    try
    {
      ++myCounter;
    }
    finally
    {
      try
```

```
        {
            Monitor.Exit(myCounterLock);
        }
        catch { }
    }
}
// ... whatever other logic ...
}
```

Example 13 Monitor.TryEnter()

The above code is very easy to understand. The *Monitor.TryEnter*() will return false if it fails to acquire the lock after timeout.

4.1.5 Thread Re-entry

A thread will be blocked while waiting for acquiring a lock. An important detail to note is that a thread will never block itself. This means if a thread owns a particular lock, it will not be blocked when it issues another *lock* or *Monitor.Enter*() methods against the same lock. This is not surprising because a lock is associated with a thread. Therefore if a thread owns a lock, it owns this lock regardless how and when this lock is acquired.

In the following example, the code will not be blocked at the *lock* statement within the *AnotherMethod*() method.

```
int myCounter = 0;
object myCounterLock = new object();


void MyThreadLogic()
{
```

```
  // ... whatever other logic ...
  lock(myCounterLock)
  {
    ++myCounter;
    AnotherMethod();
  }
  // ... whatever other logic ...
}


void AnotherMethod()
{
  lock (myCounterLock)
  {
    // ... whatever other logic ...
  }
}
```

Example 14 Thread Re-entry

Likewise, a thread can issue as many *Monitor.Enter*() calls as it wish in one execution path and not being blocked. However it is very important to remember it must issue as many *Monitor.Exit*() as it has issued *Monitor.Enter()* in order to properly release that lock.

4.1.6 Reader Lock and Writer Lock

The *Monitor* class gives us the ability to flexibly handle a situation when a lock is not immediately available for acquiring. This solves many practical issues. But sometimes it is still not enough. We will need an even finer control.

Logically, there are two basic types of locks. One is a reader lock and the other is a writer lock. The reason that we distinguish these two types of locks is for performance reasons. This is because we want to minimize unnecessary exclusiveness. As we will see soon, different types of locks may not be necessarily mutually exclusive. In another word, sometimes we may be able to allow more than one thread to access a critical resource without causing race conditions.

Firstly, we note that data readers are usually not mutually exclusive. This means, two readers can co-exist without causing any conflicts. However data writers are typically mutually exclusive if they may manipulate the same piece of data. Furthermore, data readers and writers are usually mutually exclusive too if a data reader is trying to read the same data while a data writer is trying to update that data. This is because readers may get dirty data if a data writer is updating the data.

If we name the lock that a data reader should acquire as a reader lock and the lock that a data writer should acquire as a writer lock, we can come to the following conclusions:

- Reader locks are not mutually exclusive
- Writer locks are mutually exclusive
- Reader locks and writer locks are mutually exclusive

In another word, as long as there is one thread has acquired a writer lock, all other threads regardless of their types must be blocked. But if there is no data writer thread and all threads are data readers, all threads can all be free to go ahead without being blocked.

We have mentioned earlier in section 4.1.2 that, as a principle, one lock should be associated with one piece of critical resource. This is still held in the case of reader and writer locks. In fact, there is still one physical lock that is associated with one piece of critical resource. However, here we have a specially designed lock class instead of any dummy object that we have used so far with the *lock* statement. This specially designed lock class is called *ReaderWriterLock* which is a native C# class. It provides us with the following methods:

- AcquireReaderLock
- AcquireWriterLock
- UpgradeToWriterLock
- DowngradeToReaderLock
- ReleaseReaderLock
- ReleaseWriterLock
- ReleaseLock

When we say we are to acquire a reader lock, we mean to get a logic reader lock handle from this *ReaderWriterLock* object by calling the *AcquireReaderLock()* method. Likewise, when we say we are to acquire a writer lock, we mean to get a logic writer lock handler from the very same *ReaderWriterLock* object using its *AcquireWriterLock()* method. Because both reader locks and writer locks come from the same underlying *ReaderWriterLock* object, the lock class itself can enforce their mutual exclusiveness.

In summary, a data reader should only acquire a reader lock and a data writer should only acquire a writer lock. Owning a read lock will not prevent other data readers from acquiring reader locks. But it will prevent somebody who tries to acquire a writer lock. Owning a writer lock will prevent everybody else from acquire either a reader lock or a writer lock.

The following sample code demonstrates *ReaderWriterLock*'s usage.

```csharp
class Program
{
  static void Main(string[] args)
  {
    // start the first reader
    Thread t1 = new Thread(new ThreadStart(RunAsDataReader));
    t1.Start();

    // wait for 1 sec before starting another reader
    Thread.Sleep(1000);

    // start the second reader
    Thread t2 = new Thread(new ThreadStart(RunAsDataReader));
    t2.Start();

    // start a writer
    Thread t3 = new Thread(new ThreadStart(RunAsDataWriter));
    t3.Start();

    // wait for 8 secs to make sure all previous readers have exited
    Thread.Sleep(8000);

    // start the third reader
    Thread t4 = new Thread(new ThreadStart(RunAsDataReader));
    t4.Start();

    // wrapup
    t1.Join();
    t2.Join();
    t3.Join();
    t4.Join();
  }
```

```
static void RunAsDataReader()
{
  PrintMsg("Entered RunAsDataReader() ...");
  try
  {
    myLock.AcquireReaderLock(-1);
    PrintMsg("Acquired a ReaderLock, wait for 5 seconds...");
    Thread.Sleep(5000);
  }
  finally
  {
    myLock.ReleaseReaderLock();
  }
  PrintMsg("Exit RunAsDataReader() ...");
}

static void RunAsDataWriter()
{
  PrintMsg("Entered RunAsDataWriter() ...");
  try
  {
    myLock.AcquireWriterLock(-1);
    PrintMsg("Acquired a WriterLock, wait for 5 seconds...");
    Thread.Sleep(5000);
  }
  finally
  {
    myLock.ReleaseWriterLock();
  }
  PrintMsg("Exit RunAsDataWriter() ...");
}
```

```
static void PrintMsg(String msg)
{
  Console.WriteLine("{0} - {1}", DateTime.Now, msg);
}


private static ReaderWriterLock myLock = new ReaderWriterLock();
}
```

Example 15 ReaderWriterLock

Its output is shown in the following figure. Please pay extra attention to the timestamp before every message.

```
8:55:01 PM - Entered RunAsDataReader() ...
8:55:01 PM - Acquired a ReaderLock, wait for 5 seconds...
8:55:02 PM - Entered RunAsDataReader() ...
8:55:02 PM - Entered RunAsDataWriter() ...
8:55:02 PM - Acquired a ReaderLock, wait for 5 seconds...
8:55:06 PM - Exit RunAsDataReader() ...
8:55:07 PM - Exit RunAsDataReader() ...
8:55:07 PM - Acquired a WriterLock, wait for 5 seconds...
8:55:10 PM - Entered RunAsDataReader() ...
8:55:12 PM - Exit RunAsDataWriter() ...
8:55:12 PM - Acquired a ReaderLock, wait for 5 seconds...
8:55:17 PM - Exit RunAsDataReader() ...
```

In the above sample program, *t1* and *t2* are two data readers. Therefore we can see they are not mutually excluded. However, *t3* as a data writer will be blocked until both *t1* and *t2* have exited. When *t3* owns a writer lock, it will block everybody else. Therefore *t4* as a data reader will be blocked until *t3* has exited.

To some extents, we can think a writer lock is stronger typed lock than a reader locker is. As we have mentioned earlier, both reader locks and writer locks are logical handles of a physical underlying *ReaderWriterLock* object. Therefore it is possible for a lock's owner to change the type of the lock it owns. For example, a thread that owns a reader lock can try to upgrade its lock to a writer lock. Likewise, a thread that owns a writer lock can try to downgrade its lock to a reader lock. Clearly, such flexibility is very useful in practice from performance perspective. Quite often, we have a program that spends long time on reading data and only occasionally on updating data. In such a case, it will be optimal for this thread to first acquire a reader lock and only upgrade to a writer lock when needed.

When a thread requests to upgrade a reader lock to a writer lock, the request will be immediately fulfilled if and only if it is the only thread that holds a lock (i.e. nobody else currently owns either a reader lock or a write lock). Otherwise, the upgrade request will be blocked until all other threads have released the locks that they own. However a downgrade request from a writer lock to a reader lock will usually be fulfilled immediately. These two conclusions are very easy to reach.

4.2   Avoid Deadlock

Besides race condition, another commonly seen pitfall in developing multithreaded program is deadlock. Deadlock means that several threads mutually lock each other and, as a result, all these thread will be blocked forever. This typically happens when these threads need to acquire multiple locks simultaneously but every thread only owns some of these locks and wait for the rest locks before proceed to perform their jobs. In such situation, no thread will release these locks it owns before the thread gets the chance to perform its job. This creates a vicious cycle and no thread will eventually get all locks in order to complete its task. As a result, all threads will wait for each other infinitively.

The following is a simple program example which may potentially cause deadlock.

```
object myLock1 = new object();
object myLock2 = new object();

// This function tries to acquire the 1st lock before
// the 2nd lock
public void MyFunction1()
{
  lock (myLock1)
  {
    lock (myLock2)
    {
      // ... whatever logic ....
    }
  }
}


// This function tries to acquire the 2nd lock before
// the 1st lock
public void MyFunction2()
{
  lock (myLock2)
  {
    lock (myLock1)
    {
      // ... whatever logic ....
    }
```

```
    }
}
```

Example 16 Deadlock

To see the problem in the above code, let's imagine we have two threads, *T1* and *T2*. They will call *MyFunction1()* and *MyFunction2()* respectively. If T2 has executed *lock(myLock2)* just after *T1* has executed *lock(myLock1)* but not *lock(myLock2)*, we will have a deadlock. This is because now *T1* owns *myLock1* but waits for acquiring *myLock2,* while *T2* owns *myLock2* but waits for acquiring *myLock1*. At this moment, neither of these two threads will ever acquire both locks.

T1	T2	Result
lock(myLock1)		
	lock(myLock2)	
lock(myLock2)		T1 will wait infinitively for T2 to release myLock2.
	lock(myLock1)	T2 will wait infinitively for T1 to release myLock1.

There are several practical solutions to prevent deadlock. One solution is always to use a timeout setting when making attempt to acquire a lock. In such setup, at the time of expiry, a thread will give up its attempt and releases all the locks it owns. This gives other threads chances to acquire those locks that they are waiting for. As such, no thread will end up with waiting for some locks infinitively, i.e. no deadlock will occur. However this solution will increase the complexity of the code. Firstly, we have to use *Monitor* class instead of the more convenient *lock* statement. Secondly, we also need to work out an alternative logic in case we cannot acquire a lock that we need.

A more elegant and simpler solution is for all threads to follow a predefined sequence when they need to acquire more than one lock. In the above example, for instance, we may enforce that *myLock1* must be acquired before *myLock2* can be acquired. In another word, any thread which wishes to acquire both locks must first try to acquire *myLock1* before try to acquire *myLock2*. Under this rule, we need rewrite the 2nd method as the following.

```
public void MyFunction2()
{
  lock (myLock1)
  {
    lock (myLock2)
    {
      // ... whatever logic ....
    }
  }
}
```

Now it is easy to see that the previously described deadlock will no longer occur in this situation.

4.3 Lazy Caching and Double-Checking

Locking as described in section 4.1 is important and very often essential in developing a multithreaded application. But there is no free lunch. Locking is an expensive operation. In fact, it gets more expensive when we get more CPUs on the same computer. As we know, a thread can be executed on any of the available CPUs. This implies that thread lock will require inter-CPU coordination. It is because a thread which attempts to acquire a lock will cause all CPUs to check whether this attempt should be granted. We know that inter-CPU coordination is an expensive operation. As such we can conclude that, for the performance reason, we should avoid locking whenever it is possible and safe to do.

There are many different strategies which can help achieve this goal. This section will just discuss one of these, known as double-checking pattern. This pattern is commonly used in conjunction with a so called lazy caching strategy. The reason we choose this is because lazy caching is widely used in front office applications. It will be used again in section 4.4 when we discuss how to eliminate unnecessary locking. The technique discussed in that section is very practical and effective in developing some high performance real-time front office applications.

Let's first talk about lazy caching technique.

Many front office analytic libraries are basically number producers. To produce some numbers will require certain computation efforts. Sometimes, these numbers may be used repeatedly millions of times or even more. A good example is discount factors as predicted by an interest rate yield curve. Even though calculating one number once usually is not that expensive on a modern computer, repeating millions of times may be a different story. Therefore a common practice is to calculate once and then to store the result in a cache for later use.

There are two ways to populate a cache. One is to pre-calculate all the data and populate the whole cache once before any of these data can be requested. The other is to calculate and populate the cache on-demand. This means that when the program starts, the cache is empty. When one piece of data is requested, it will be calculated on-the-fly and then stored in the cache. When more and more data have been requested, the cache will start being filled up. Even though the cache may not necessarily be completely filled up, all the data that have been requested at least once will be cached. The 1st approach is sometime called pre-caching. The 2nd approach is often called lazy caching.

To some extents, from development perspective, pre-caching may be somewhat slightly cleaner and easier. But comparison of practical benefits between these two approaches depends on the expected usage profile of these data. If almost all data will be requested (such as in the case of running a long batch job), the cache will be almost completely filled up during job execution anyway. Therefore in such cases, pre-caching may make more sense. However, in other cases when only a small portion of the data will be requested, lazy caching will clearly offer more performance gain by avoiding unnecessary computation of those unused data.

Many real-time applications offer good examples when lazy-caching technique makes more sense. For example, in a real-time pricing application, a market reference object (such as a yield curve etc) is constructed based on real-time market data (e.g. from Bloomberg or Reuters etc). During market active time, a snapshot of such reference data may quickly become obsolete. This implies a market reference object, such a yield curve, has a very short life-time. As such, it is very likely that only a small amount of data will be used before this yield curve retires.

The nature of lazy caching is to produce a piece of data on-demand.

Therefore, quite often we have to consider potential multithreading issues. This is because if there are several client applications or any of client applications is multithreading enabled, we may get multiple requests from different threads simultaneously. If these requests happen to request exactly the same piece of data, we may have to ensure only one of them will trigger the calculation and store the result to the cache. All the other should retrieve the result from the cache.

From coding perspective, the following does NOT do exactly what we want. This is because even though it can guarantee one and only one thread can perform calculation and stores the data into the cache at a time, it will result in all threads repeating the same actions. Even though the lock will prevent multiple threads from entering the calculation code simultaneously, it essentially enforces all threads to enter this logic in a sequential manner.

```
acquire_lock
{
    // performs calculation and stores the result into cache
}
```

To avoid repeated calculation, we can implement the following logic:

```
acquire_lock
{
    if(!data_is_processed)
    {
        // performs calculation and stores the result into cache
        data_is_processed = true;
    }
}
```

```
}
```

The *data_is_processed* is a flag which indicates whether the data has been calculated. There is a one-to-one mapping between a piece of data and a flag. A flag's initial value is false. After a piece of data has been produced, its corresponding flag's value will be set to true. Please note that it is not necessary to have a flag as a separate boolean value. Sometimes we can initialize the data in the cache to an invalid value (e.g. *NaN*) to indicate they have not been processed. When a piece of data has been calculated, it will contain a valid number. As a result we can know whether a piece of data has been calculated by testing whether it contains an invalid value.

The pseudo code shown above works, but it has some room for improvement. The code below is an improved version by using the so-called double-checking pattern.

```
if (!data_is_processed)
{
    acquire_lock
    {
        if(!data_is_processed)
        {
            // performs calculation and stores the result into cache
            data_is_processed = true;
        }
    }
}
```

Example 17 Double-Checking

The first check statement is to avoid unnecessary locking because, as explained previously, locking is an expensive operation. Without the 1st check, all data requests must always acquire a lock which is clearly unnecessary when the data has been produced already. The 2nd check statement is to avoid repeated calculation. To see this, let's assume we have two threads, *T1* and *T2*, and the requested piece of data has not been calculated (i.e. *data_is_processed* is false). If *T2* kicks in any time before *T1* set *data_is_processed* to be true, it will pass the first check statement and be blocked when trying to acquire the lock. After *T1* sets the *data_is_processed* to true and releases the lock, *T2* will get the lock and enter the inside logic. If we do not have the 2nd check statement, *T2* will perform the calculation again!

Again, double-checking is one of the most commonly used design patterns in developing multithreaded applications. We will almost for sure see it in many front office applications.

4.4 Eliminate Unnecessary Locking – A Practical Example

The previous example of double checking essentially use a cheaper *if* statement to avoiding some unnecessary locking. This helps improve the performance. But this design still requires locking at least once per calculation of every piece of request data. In section 4.1, we have explained that locking is necessary to avoid race condition by ensuring only one thread can manipulate critical resource at a time.

But the question is what if the result is always deterministic even if several threads are manipulating the critical resource simultaneously with unpredictable executing sequence? This turns out to be a very practical question. This is because if there is no race condition involved, we may avoid using some locking. It is undoubtedly that a lock-free implementation will give us a meaningful performance boost.

Many front office analytic libraries use deterministic algorithms. This means if the input is given, the output is deterministic. For example, if an interest rate yield curve has been constructed using a given set of market data inputs, all discount factors implied by this yield curve will be deterministic. If we use *df(t)* to denote the discount factor for time *t*, *df(t)* is deterministic regardless of how many times and when we try to calculate its value as long as the curve itself has not been reconstructed using a different set of market data.

In such case (i.e. the result is guaranteed to be deterministic) it turns out that we can eliminate all the locking and still be able to have a thread-safe implementation.

The following sample code uses a classic double-checking pattern with lock. All the data in the discount factor cache, i.e. myCache, have been initialized to 0 (which is an invalid value for a discount factor). The implementation is very simple and straight-forward.

```
public double GetDiscountFactor(int t)
{
  double df = myCache[t];
  if (0 == df) // df(t) is not calculated & set to the cache
  {
    lock (myLock) // ← can we eliminate this?
    {
      df = myCache[t];
      if (0 == df) // df(t) is still not calculated & set to the
                   // cache
```

```
        {
            // calculate the df
            myCache[t] = df;

        }

    }

  }

  return df;

}
private double[] myCache; // cache, all initialized to 0.0
private object myLock;     // lock
```

The following code segment is a simplified version of the previous code but this version does not use any lock.

```
public double GetDiscountFactor(int t)
{
  double df = myCache[t];
  if (0 == df) // df(t) is not calculated & set to the cache
  {
    // calculate the df
    myCache[t] = df;
  }
  return df;
}
private double[] myCache; // cache, all initialized to 0.0
```

Example 18 Eliminating Unnecessary Locking

In the above simplified version, we bear the potential cost of duplicated calculation of some discount factors if they are requested by several threads simultaneously. But the important point is that the final result is always deterministic. By bearing the potential cost of duplicated calculation, we can eliminate all the locks and their associated cost. In practice, this usually produces a meaningful net positive performance gain. This is because simultaneous requesting of exactly the same discount factor is very rare. As such, the cost of repeated calculation often can be ignored. But on the other hand, if we use the classic double-check pattern, we will for sure incur the cost of one lock per piece of data's calculation. Clearly its cost usually far out-weights that of potential duplicated calculation.

We must emphasize that the reason why we can eliminate the lock is because the result is deterministic. Otherwise we must use lock as a safe guard. We also need to point out here, in this example we will not mess up memory either because discount factors are simply double values. If there is risk of messing up memory (quite often in the case of using raw pointers in C++), we may still have to use lock in order to avoid memory leaks.

4.5 Double-Buffer Pattern - A Practical Example

Double-buffer pattern is often seen in graphic programming where two image buffers are maintained. One of them is visible i.e. its contents are displayed on screen. The other is invisible. The benefit of such design is that we can manipulate the data behind the scene by using the invisible buffer. After the data process is completed, we then switch the two buffers and make the latest image to be visible instantly as a whole. This is especially useful when the image process is somewhat complicated. If we use only one visible buffer, we may risk some image delay and/or blinks visible to the users. As a result, this double-buffer design can be very effective in improving users' visual experience.

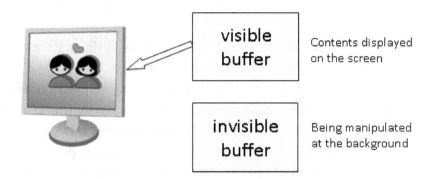

visible buffer — Contents displayed on the screen

invisible buffer — Being manipulated at the background

Interestingly, this double-buffer design pattern can also be applied to develop front office applications. It is particularly useful in writing multithreaded real-time applications that use real time market data.

Let's continue using an interest rate yield curve library as an example. We know that an interest rate yield curve is constructed using real time market data. This means if market data changes, this yield curve will need to be reconstructed. However, from users' perspective, we must satisfy many requirements. Some of these requirements are listed below:

1. Portfolio/Cash-flow valuation must be internally consistent. This means that the yield curve that is used for pricing cannot be changed during evaluation process. This is critically important because otherwise we may end up with a situation where different parts of the same portfolio or cash-flow are evaluated using different curves.
2. A new yield curve must be constructed as soon as possible after new market data is received. This is an important requirement because using an obsolete curve is clearly very dangerous and

may open ourselves to be arbitraged.
3. A new pricing request should have access to the latest yield curve (i.e. the curve built with latest market data).

Now let's assume we only have one curve in the system and examine what difficulties we will face in this design. In this case, the current curve must be locked when a new pricing request comes in (e.g. a request to price a big portfolio). This is to satisfy the 1st requirement as described above. Therefore before this portfolio valuation process has been done, this curve cannot be changed (i.e. re-constructed) even if new market data become available. As a result, any new pricing requests will have to use this curve because it is the latest curve we have in the system. This contradicts to the 3rd requirement.

In fact, the situation will turn out to be nastier than we may think. If we have pricing requests coming in continuously, the curve may be kept locked for an extended period without any opportunity of being reconstructed. This is because all the pricing requests only need to acquire reader locks (see section 4.1.6). A reader lock does not prevent others from acquiring another reader lock. As such, other pricing requests can come in. But a reader lock will prevent others from acquiring writer locks. Therefore if we have pricing requests come in continuously, we may end up with a situation that the curve is kept locked. As a result, even if there are new market data become available, we may have no chance to reconstruct the curve. Clearly this is not desirable.

On the other hand, if we actively prevent some pricing requests from acquiring the current curve immediately just in order to have some opportunities to reconstruct the curve, we may cause unnecessary delays in serving those pricing requests. In fact, this strategy is not very efficient because we cannot foresee for sure when new market data will become available. Therefore we may end up holding off pricing requests for no real benefits. What's more critical is this strategy does not solve the problem when there is a long-running pricing request which locks the curve for an extended period.

One solution to address this issue is to use a pattern that is similar to the double buffer pattern. In this case, a buffer is a curve. The visible curve is the latest curve. At any time, there is only one visible curve. Meanwhile, there may be several invisible curves that exist in the system. An invisible curve can be either a curve-in-building (i.e. a newer curve that is being constructed using newly available market data) or a retired obsolete curve (i.e. a curve that is older than the current visible curve but is still used by somebody). We will explain later why a retired curve may still exist in the system. In summary, in this design, we may have several curves co-existing in the system, not necessarily two curves.

Whenever a pricing request comes in, it will be given the current visible curve. Because the current curve is the latest available curve, the 2nd requirement as described above will be satisfied. When new market data becomes available, a new curve will be created. Before this new curve construction is completed, it remains invisible. But as soon as the construction has completed, this new curve will be switched on and become visible. At this point, the previously visible curve will be switched off and becomes invisible. One interesting thing here is that all objects are essentially smart pointers in C#. This means if somebody still holds a handle to this curve, this curve object will be not destroyed even if it becomes invisible. And if nobody holds its handler, the curve will be automatically destroyed and garbage collected. This is a very important feature to satisfy the 1st requirement above. Let's imagine a big portfolio comes in and is given the current curve for pricing purpose. While evaluation is still in progress, some new market data becomes available. As already described, a newer curve will be constructed using these new market data. It will be switched on after the building process has completed. At this moment, the curve that this portfolio holds will become invisible but still available for the portfolio to use. As such, we can guarantee the portfolio evaluation will be internally consistent. After the portfolio evaluation process has completed, it will drop its handle to that curve. At this point, if nobody else holds this curve, this invisible curve will be automatically destroyed.

The following figure shows a high level design of the system. The *GetCurve()* interface is the single point of access for users to request a curve object. This method will always return the current visible, i.e. the most up to date curve.

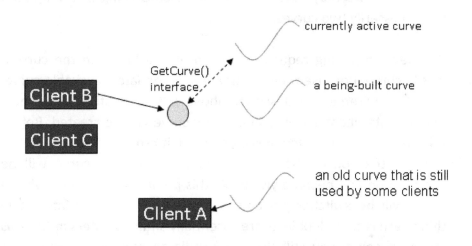

Figure 7 Double Buffer Pattern Used in Curve Building

From technical implementation perspective, it is easy to see that this design requires almost similar efforts as the single curve design. To some extents, this design may be even simpler and more modular than the single curve design. It is because that the threading locking mechanism is much cleaner and much less pervasive in a "double buffer" design than in a single curve design.

The following sample code segment is a framework skeleton which demonstrates this "double buffer" design:

```
public class DoubleBufferSample
{
  private ICurve myLatestCurve;

  public ICurve GetCurve()
  {
    return myLatestCurve;
  }

  private void BuildCurve()
  {
    ICurve curveInConstruction;
    // build curveInConstruction
    // assign curveInConstruction to myLatestCurve;
  }
}
```

Example 19 Double Buffer Design Code Skeleton

4.6 Thread Synchronization

Even though logically a thread is an atomic entity, it cannot exist by itself. It must be owned by somebody such as a process or another thread. When a thread is started, it is possible for its owner to inspect its general status (i.e. running, paused etc) and terminate it by brutal force when needed. However it usually will be difficult for its owner or another thread to control and communicate with a running thread. Some seemingly simple thread control operations such as suspending and resuming a thread are in fact somewhat much more complicated than we first think. In the latest version of .NET framework, both the *Thread.Suspend*() and *Thread.Resume*() methods have been marked as obsolete, even though both methods look intuitive (I guess this is the reason why they were available from earlier version of .NET framework in the first place). The reason that it may be risky to suspend a thread forcefully from outside is because an outsider is unable to know the internal status of a thread. Thus, it may leave the running thread in an internally messy status by suspending it forcefully. The correct way to perform these operations is to communicate with that thread using signal so that that thread performs these operations voluntarily. In another word, an outsider should send a signal to the running thread in question. Then it is up to that running thread to decide how to respond this signal (such as by suspending itself). A comparable real life example is something like one person asks his colleague "can I use your computer?" That person may response by "just a minute, let me save my document first and then you can have the computer." Clearly it will be a very bad habit for the requestor to forcefully push his college away without giving him a chance to wrap up what he is currently doing.

If we think in details, thread synchronization has two aspects. One is to share data and the other is to coordinate execution flow control. The first one solves how to exchange data information among different threads. And the other solves how to make different threads run in a cooperative and controlled manner.

In this section we assume all the threads are owned and running within the same process. In another word, we are going to discuss intra-process threads synchronization. Inter-process synchronization will be discussed in section 4.8.

4.6.1 Share Data

To share data among different threads is relatively simple. What we need to do is to pass the same piece of data among different threads so that everybody can see and have access to this data.

If any of these threads may change this piece of shared data, we will have the same concern as critical resource protection that has been described in section 4.1. However, in practice, vast majority of such cases is a much simpler scenario. The owner of the thread just simply wants to pass in some input parameters for the thread to work on. When this thread has completed its job, the owner will retrieve the result. In such case, we can be sure that data updating (by the thread) will not happen at the same time as data reading (by the owner). Therefore we don't need to worry about potential race condition.

To pass in data to a thread is simple. Among others, one way is to pass the data into the thread class construction like what we have done in the thread example given in section 7.2 of the previous book *C# in Front Office*. For convenient purpose, we have copied a segment of the code below:

```
MyWorker w1 = new MyWorker("Tom");
Thread t1 = new Thread(new ThreadStart(w1.DoJob));
```

MyWorker is a regular class which has a constructor taking a string as the parameter. It has also defined a *void DoJob()* method which can be used to construct a thread. If we have passed a string ("*Tom*" in this example) in the constructor, we will be able to use it in the *DoJob*() method.

We can also modify the above code to something like the following:

```
SomeDataType myData = new SomeDataType();
// populate the myData
MyWorker w1 = new MyWorker(myData);
Thread t1 = new Thread(new ThreadStart(w1.DoJob));
t1.Join();
// inspect the myData
```

Example 20 Exchange Data Information with a Thread

It is easy to see that we can stuff the *myData* member with some initial input parameters. The thread can update this *myData* during its execution. After the thread execution completes (after the *Join*() method), we will be able to inspect *myData* and retrieve the output.

4.6.2 Synchronize Execution Flow

To synchronize execution flow is more complicated than to share data. When we are sharing data among different threads, threads has the control. This means that it is up to the thread to decide when and how to read the data. But when we are coordinating several threads, threads may be the subjects that are being controlled. This means that a suspended thread needs to be woke up by something else.

The basic logical concept behind thread synchronization is actually quite simple. Two threads can coordinate between themselves by sending and receiving signals. After having received a signal, a thread can decide to suspend itself and wait for a signal to wake it up. This signal is usually sent by another thread. Below is a simple sample which demonstrates the basic thread synchronization technique.

```csharp
using System;
using System.Threading;

class Program
{
  static void Main(string[] args)
  {
    AutoResetEvent signal = new AutoResetEvent(false);
    MyWorker worker1 = new MyWorker(signal);
    Thread t1 = new Thread(new ThreadStart(worker1.Run));
    t1.Start();
    Thread.Sleep(10 * 1000);
    signal.Set();
    t1.Join();
  }
}

public class MyWorker
{
  public MyWorker(AutoResetEvent signal)
  {
    mySignal = signal;
  }

  public void Run()
  {
    Console.WriteLine("[{0}] Worker waits for signal.",
```

```
DateTime.Now);
    mySignal.WaitOne();
    Console.WriteLine("[{0}] Worker wakes up.", DateTime.Now);
  }
  private AutoResetEvent mySignal;
}
```

Example 21 Thread Synchronization

The example above is easy to understand. The main program starts a thread. This thread will wait for the main program to send a signal before continue. The signal is sent using an *AutoResetEvent* object. This *AutoResetEvent* class has two statuses: signaled and un-signaled. When it is constructed, the *false* parameter is to set its initial status to un-signaled. Therefore the thread will have to wait for its status becomes signaled. The main program will wait for 10 seconds before setting its status to be signaled. At that time, the thread will be waken up and continue its execution.

The following figure shows the execution result:

```
[4/13/2010 6:22:40 PM] Worker waits for signal.
[4/13/2010 6:22:50 PM] Worker wakes up.
```

In this example, the signal is sent between a thread and its owner (the main program). The same technique can be used to synchronize two independent threads.

Sometimes, we may need to synchronize more than two threads. For example, one thread may want to wait for several other threads to signal before continue. This scenario is very relevant to Monte Carlo simulation which we will have a detailed discussion in the next section.

In the following example, the main program creates four threads and waits for all of them to signal before exit.

```
using System;
using System.Threading;

namespace MutexSample
{
  class Program
  {
    public static void Main(string[] args)
    {
      int noOfThreads = 4;
      AutoResetEvent[] signals = new AutoResetEvent[noOfThreads];
      Thread[] threads = new Thread[noOfThreads];
      for (int ii = 0; ii < noOfThreads; ++ii)
      {
        AutoResetEvent signal = new AutoResetEvent(false);
        MyWorker worker = new MyWorker(ii + 1, signal);
        Thread t = new Thread(new ThreadStart(worker.Run));
        signals[ii] = signal;
        threads[ii] = t;
        t.Start();
      }

      AutoResetEvent.WaitAll(signals);
```

```csharp
      Console.WriteLine("main program exits.");
    }
}


public class MyWorker
{
  public MyWorker(int seq, AutoResetEvent signal)
  {
    mySeq = seq;
    mySignal = signal;
  }


  public void Run()
  {
     Thread.Sleep(mySeq * 1000);
     Console.WriteLine("Thread {0} signals.", mySeq);
     mySignal.Set();
  }


  private int mySeq;
  private AutoResetEvent mySignal;
  }
}
```

Example 22 Thread Synchroniztion (more than 2 threads)

Running this program will produce the following result:

```
Thread 1 signals.
Thread 2 signals.
Thread 3 signals.
Thread 4 signals.
main program exits.
```

Please note that in this example, we can simply use *Join*() method instead. Using the *Join*() method has been discussed in the previous book *C# in Front Office*. This method allows us to wait for all threads to complete and exit. To some extents, we can view *Join*() method as waiting for thread exit events. If we want all threads to be still alive after signaling and continue executing upon receiving another signal (as often the case in Monte Carlos simulation), we cannot use the *Join*() method. Instead we have to use the technique as shown in this example.

The *AutoResetEvent.WaitAll*() method will block the current thread until all *AutoResetEvents* objects have signaled. Alternatively, we can use the *AutoResetEvent.WaitAny*() method. This method will block the current thread until at least one *AutoResetEvent* has signaled. If we use *AutoResetEvent.WaitAny*() instead of *AutoResetEvent.WaitAll*() that is used in Example 22, we may see the following result:

```
Thread 1 signals.
main program exits.
Thread 2 signals.
Thread 3 signals.
Thread 4 signals.
```

Finally, we are introducing a more complex but at the same time more practical example. This example will demonstrate how to implement two-way synchronization between a main program and several threads. In the code sample below, the main program creates and starts four threads. It will then wait for all of these threads to signal. This part is similar to that in Example 22. What's different is that in this example, the four threads will then wait for the main program to send back a signal before continue its own execution.

This example essentially gives a simplified implementation of a Monte Carlo simulation which will be discussed in the next section.

```
using System;
using System.Threading;

namespace MutexSample
{
  class Program
  {
    public static void Main(string[] args)
    {
      int noOfThreads = 4;
      AutoResetEvent[] signals = new AutoResetEvent[noOfThreads];
      AutoResetEvent[] signals2 = new AutoResetEvent[noOfThreads];
      Thread[] threads = new Thread[noOfThreads];
      for (int ii = 0; ii < noOfThreads; ++ii)
      {
        AutoResetEvent signal = new AutoResetEvent(false);
        AutoResetEvent signal2 = new AutoResetEvent(false);
        MyWorker worker = new MyWorker(ii + 1, signal, signal2);
        Thread t = new Thread(new ThreadStart(worker.Run));
        signals[ii] = signal;
        signals2[ii] = signal2;
```

```csharp
      threads[ii] = t;
      t.Start();
    }

    AutoResetEvent.WaitAll(signals);
    Console.WriteLine("main program is doing something.");
    Thread.Sleep(3 * 1000);
    foreach (AutoResetEvent a in signals2)
    {
      a.Set();
    }
    Console.WriteLine("main program waits for all threads to
complete.");
    foreach (Thread t in threads)
    {
      t.Join();
    }
    Console.WriteLine("main proram exits.");
  }
}


public class MyWorker
{
  public MyWorker(int seq, AutoResetEvent signal, AutoResetEvent
signal2)
  {
    mySeq = seq;
    mySignal = signal;
    mySignal2 = signal2;
  }

  public void Run()
```

```
   {
      Thread.Sleep(mySeq * 1000);
      Console.WriteLine("Thread {0} signals.", mySeq);
      mySignal.Set();
      Console.WriteLine("Thread {0} waiting for signal ...",
mySeq);
      mySignal2.WaitOne();
      Console.WriteLine("Thread {0} received the signal ...",
mySeq);
   }

   private int mySeq;
   private AutoResetEvent mySignal, mySignal2;
  }
}
```

Example 23 Thread Synchronization (Two-Way)

Executing the above sample code will produce the following result.

```
Thread 1 signals.
Thread 1 waiting for signal ...
Thread 2 signals.
Thread 2 waiting for signal ...
Thread 3 signals.
Thread 3 waiting for signal ...
Thread 4 signals.
Thread 4 waiting for signal ...
main program is doing something.
main program waits for all threads to complete.
Thread 1 received the signal ...
Thread 3 received the signal ...
Thread 2 received the signal ...
Thread 4 received the signal ...
main proram exits.
```

4.7   Monte Carlo

Monte Carlo simulation is probably one of the most important techniques that are used in many front office analytic libraries. It is widely used in numerical procedure based calibration, pricing and other similar processes. Arguably, Monte Carlo simulation is also the most expensive financial computation that is commonly seen in a front office environment.

Monte Carlo is a powerful way to study random events. It does so by simulating tens of thousands or even millions of different scenarios and then studying the results under these different scenarios. Many complex financial products' payoffs depend on unpredictable future events. In many cases, there are no close-formed analytic formulas to price these products. Monte Carlo can be a powerful way to price these products. Monte Carlo's basic approach is to price a financial product under different future scenarios and then analyze those results in order to get a theoretical price. Typically, the more different scenarios it generates, the more accurate the result will be in theory. The need to simulate large number of different scenarios makes Monte Carlos a very expensive procedure.

One interesting feature that we may notice in using Monte Carlos is that all scenarios are mostly independent to each other. This means that we can run several scenario simulations simultaneously without interfering each other. As such, multi-threading is a natural technical fit to implement Monte Carlo simulation. That is, we can use one thread to simulate one scenario and execute multiple threads to simulate multiple scenarios simultaneously.

This said, in practice, Monte Carlo simulation will sometime require periodical data rebalance among different scenarios. This is because each scenario in a Monte Carlos simulation will need some reference data. These data usually need to satisfy certain statistical distribution such as normal or log-normal distribution. After these initial data have been processed under different scenarios, some new data may be produced. We often need to enforce those new data to conform certain distribution too. Therefore, we may have to adjust these new data. This is what we referred earlier as rebalance. Technically, this implies that all simulation threads may have to synchronize among themselves during the process. Figure 8 below shows a simplified technical view of a typical Monte Carlos process.

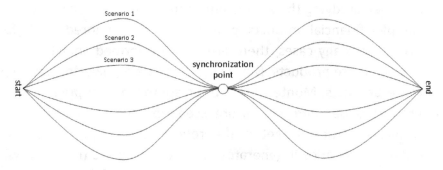

Figure 8 Monte Carlo

In the above figure, each line stands for one particular simulation path (technically one thread). At the beginning of simulation, the main program (i.e. the simulation controller) will create several threads and assign initial data to each of them. These threads will then run independently until reaching a synchronization point. At this point, the simulation controller will inspect data of all these threads and adjust them accordingly before letting all the threads continue executing. Finally after all threads have finished, the simulation controller will inspect all the data and retrieve the result for further processing.

Now it is clear that Example 23 on page 94 shows a program skeleton of Monte Carlos simulation. It has the logic to create and kick off all these threads, synchronize these threads in the middle and then wait for all threads to complete. In terms of data that is needed in Monte Carlos simulation, one simple and intuitive design is to create an array of data each of which maps to one scenario (thread). One piece of data element contains input data, all intermediate data and final result. At the beginning of the process, the simulation controller will populate the input data before kicking off all these threads. Each thread will then produce some intermediate data during its process. At a synchronization point, the simulation controller can inspect those intermediate data and perform necessary readjustment. At the end of a simulation, a thread will populate this data with final result. The simulation controller will then be able to collect all such results and calculate a final price (e.g. by averaging etc).

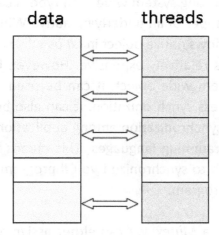

Figure 9 Monte Carlo - Mapping between Data and Thread

4.8   Inter-Process Synchronization

4.8.1   Synchronize Execution Flow

So far all we have discussed is how to synchronize different threads within one process. An *AutoResetEvent* object is also a piece of data. Therefore, intra-process thread synchronization is achieved by having a process wide object that is accessible to all threads within that process. However this approach will not work in inter-process thread synchronization because a process has no access to a piece of data that lives within another process. In order to make a piece of data visible to several processes, this data must exist at the operating system level. Therefore, if we want to implement inter-process signal, we need an operating system wide signal object.

In C#, this operating system wide data type is called *Mutex*. In fact, a *Mutex* is a wrapper of an underlying native Windows object. Using a wrapped Windows native object in C# usually is expensive. Therefore using *Mutex* is relatively expensive. However, because *Mutex* is an operating system wide object, it can be used in both intra-process and inter-process synchronization. It can also be used to implement inter-process synchronization among applications that are written in different programming languages. This means that we can use the same approach to synchronize two C# programs or one C# program and one C++ program.

When creating a *Mutex*, we can either assign a string name to it or do not assign a name to it. The latter is called unnamed *Mutex*. An unnamed *Mutex* is only visible to the process that it resides. In another word, it is a local *Mutex*. A local *Mutex* can only be used in synchronizing different threads within a process, not cross processes. We have no interests in a local *Mutex* here because we already have other native C# classes for intra-process synchronization. An example is the *Monitor* class that has been discussed in section 4.1.4 on page 57.

If a *Mutex* is created with a name, it is called a named *Mutex*. A named *Mutex* is visible throughout the whole operating system. We are interested in named *Mutex* here. Please note that it is possible to further control a named *Mutex*'s scope of visibility by using different formatted string as its name. This is a very important point in certain scenario such as running applications in a Windows terminal service. These features are fully documented in MSDN. Here we will only demonstrate the most basic usage of named *Mutexes*.

The following is a sample program that shows how to use a named *Mutex* to synchronize multiple processes. It is intuitive to understand that a named *Mutex* is indentified by its name. Therefore as long as different processes get hold of a named *Mutex* with the same name, these processes have access to the same *Mutex*. As such, they can signal with each other by manipulating this named *Mutex*.

```csharp
class Program
{
  static void Main(string[] args)
  {
    myName = DateTime.Now.Minute, DateTime.Now.Second);
    PrintMessage("started.");

    bool requestInitialOwnerShip = true;
    bool isCreated;
    Mutex myMutex = new Mutex(requestInitialOwnerShip
```

```
                    , "MyMutexSample"
                    , out isCreated
                );

    if (!isCreated)
    {
      PrintMessage("is blocked, waiting ...");
      myMutex.WaitOne();
    }

    PrintMessage("has the mutext, executing some logic.");
    Thread.Sleep(1000 * 60);
    PrintMessage("Exit.");
    myMutex.ReleaseMutex();
  }

  private static void PrintMessage(String msg)
  {
    Console.WriteLine("[{0}] {1} {2}", DateTime.Now, myName, msg);
  }

  private static String myName;
}
```

Example 24 Inter-Process Synchronization: Named Mutex

If we execute this program in two different command windows, the output will look similar to the following figure:

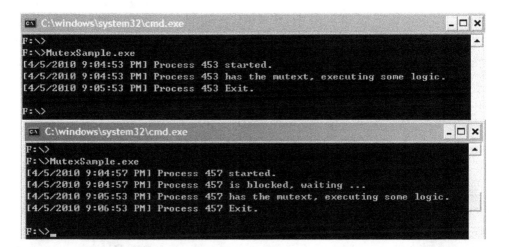

If we exam the timestamp of every printed message, we can see that the 2nd process was indeed blocked by the 1st process. In another word, a named *Mutex* indeed can help us to implement inter-process synchronization.

Similar to the *Monitor* class, a *Mutex* must be released the exactly the same number of times as it has been acquired. Otherwise that *Mutex* will be left in a so-called abandoned status. This will trigger an exception to be thrown when another process tries to acquire this *Mutex*. Abandoned *Mutex* is a serious programming error.

4.8.2 Share Data

In intra-process synchronization, sharing data is relatively easier than synchronizing execution flow. But in inter-process synchronization, to share data is relatively more troublesome than to synchronize execution flow.

There are different ways to share data among different processes.

Some are very primitive. For example, we can always share data among different processes using files or databases. Such techniques have been used for a very long time. They are relatively simple but less efficient.

Another somewhat equally matured but more efficient technique to share data among different processes is to use socket based communication. For example, TCP/IP communication, UDP broadcast or Microsoft specific .NET remoting. All of them have been discussed in the chapter 5 of the previous book, *C# in Front Office*. Another similar technique is called named pipe. It is a Windows proprietary technology which is fully documented in MSDN. We will not go into details here.

A third choice is to use so-called shared memory. It is similar to the named *Mutex* in that shared memory is also an operating system level data structure. Because it is at operating system level, it can be accessed by all processes. Therefore it can be used to exchange information among different processes. Shared memory is natively supported by Windows. We can use this facility by invoking relevant Windows APIs. In C# terminology, shared memory is called mapped files. In a simplest way, mapped file technique is to simulate a block of memory as a file. To use mapped file in C#, a thread should first use *CreateFileMapping*() to create a named mapping file and then use *MapViewOfFile*() to access it. Technically, while shared memory usually is more efficient than other approaches, we need to note the following points:

- Shared memory usually does not support complex data structure. This is because it basically offers an unstructured data blob. If applications need to share concrete objects, object serialization and de-serialization usually will be required.

-   Using shared memory implicitly disallow distributing applications to different computers. This may have some negative impact on application's scalability.

There are some examples in MSDN and elsewhere on the internet to demonstrate how to use mapped files in C#. Technically they are a little bit involved. In reality, requirements that will force us to use shared memory are somewhat rare. Therefore we will not expand further here.

4.9 Debug a Multithreaded Application

Debugging a multithreaded program is difficult and sometime very confusing. This is because the execution point will jump among different threads due to the nature of multithreading. It will become even more confusing when several threads are executing the same source code. Let's use the following code as an example:

```
public class MyWorkerExample
{
  public static void Main()
  {
    MyWorkerExample w1 = new MyWorkerExample();
    MyWorkerExample w2 = new MyWorkerExample();
    Thread t1 = new Thread(new ThreadStart(w1.Run));
    Thread t2 = new Thread(new ThreadStart(w2.Run));
    t1.Start();
    t2.Start();
    t1.Join();
    t2.Join();
    return;
```

```
    }

    public void Run()
    {
      statement_1;
      statement_2;
      statement_3;

    }

  }
```

After both threads have started, if the current statement stops at *statement_1*, we cannot easily distinguish between whether we are in thread *t1* or thread *t2*.

Fortunately, Visual Studio provides us with a thread debugging tool. It is somewhat less known and not often used, but very useful during a multithreaded program debug session. We can launch this thread inspect dialogue by selecting the thread menu from the debug toolbar, as shown below:

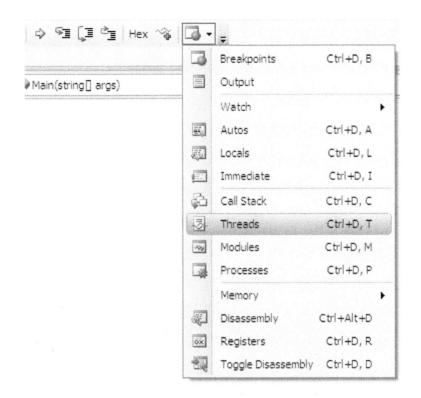

This will bring up the following dialogue which lists all the currently running thread. It also shows the current to-be-executed statement as well as every thread's current executing point.

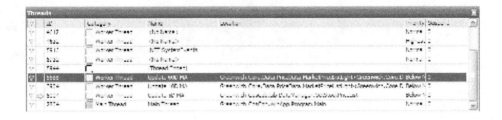

In practice, it is often quite useful to assign each thread a meaningful name. This name will be displayed in the *Name* column of the thread inspect dialogue. It gives the developer the ability to identify specific thread easily. To assign a name to a thread in C# is very easy. It can be done by setting the thread's *Name* property.

5 Develop Client Applications

5.1 Overview and Design Guideline

Front office applications usually have quite complex user interfaces. Typically these user interfaces will need to display lots of numbers and, quite often, charts. What makes front office client applications somewhat special is that Excel is a widely used client interfaces. On trading floors, Excel is not only used by itself as an electronic calculation workbook, but also used as a front end of a complex n-tier application. For example, in chapter 6 of the previous book, Excel is used as a monitoring tool for pricing and risk results.

From technical design perspective, front office applications are not much different from other types of applications. One good design principle is separation of different layers. As we will see soon, this design is very practical and useful in a front office environment.

A typical 3-tier technical architecture is shown below. It separates a system into 3 different layers: presentation, logic and data.

presentation
logic
data

A typical front office application may get data from a wide choice of sources, such as databases, flat files, real-time market data feed etc. How to develop an optimized and flexible data layer is not the focus of this chapter.

The logic layer is responsible for implementing application's business logic. C# is a full featured general purpose programming language with built-in support for many advanced techniques such as multiple threading, distributed computing etc. Therefore it is an excellent choice of implementing business logics.

The presentation layer is responsible for user interaction which includes both displaying information to users and taking user inputs. As we all know, C# is an excellent choice of implementing both rich and thin client interfaces. It also provides powerful native support to rapidly developed desktop applications, web applications and so on.

How to develop all these individual layers is not the focus of this chapter. These have been extensively discussed in many other books. Instead, in this book, we will emphasize separation of the logic and the presentation layers. This will help us to maximize efficiency and flexibility. The focus of this chapter is to discuss and solve some practical technical issues in integrating presentation layers and logic layers. This is an important topic in practice especially when the two layers are implemented using different technologies.

Before moving forward, we need to point out that the tiered design and the topics we will discuss here apply to both traditional desktop applications and distributed applications. Clearly, distributed application is getting more and more acceptance in reality, including in front office environments. Chapter 6 of the previous book, *C# in Front Office*, gives a practical example of a distributed pricing and risk calculation system that is commonly seen in a typical front office environment. In addition to distributed computing, multi-channel delivery is also very relevant in front office application development. For example, contents that are produced by one application may need to be delivered to different types of user interfaces such as desktop applications written in VB or C#, web client, Excel and even through some programmable interfaces. In such situations, it is even more important to separate different layers and pay attention to related integration issues.

The following figure shows a typical sample physical view of a 3-tiered architecture. Please note that within each block, there may be many different choices. For example, the C# block in presentation layer may be a C# desktop application, a Windows service or something else.

Excel	C#	VB	Web	Programmable API
logic				
Database		Messaging	Remote Data Source	

Figure 10 Tiered Architecture

The business logic layer can be implemented using many different languages. In this chapter, we will assume that this business logic layer is implemented using C#. Based on this, we will discuss the integration issues with presentation layers that are implemented using different languages.

5.2   C# Solution Structure

It is often a good idea to have a multi-project solution instead of a single project solution when developing a front office system using C#. A recommended solution structure is shown below:

Name	Project Type	Description
AppLib	Library	Contains business logic
WinApp	Windows Application	Executable running as a Windows application
WinService	Windows Service Application	Executable running as a standard Windows service
WebService	Web Service	Provides web service interface
WebApp	ASP .NET	A web application
COM Wrapper	Library	Provides interface to Excel and Visual Basic client

Example 25 Recommended C# Solution Structure

Usually the heaviest project is the *AppLib* project which contains all the business logic. It may or may not include relevant data layer implementation. All the other projects will reference to this *AppLib* project therefore are able to access business logic. Each of these projects implements a specific presentation layer interface. For example, a *WinApp* project contains some windows form related controls and builds a Windows application. A WinService project contains window service controller and builds a Windows service application. A COM wrapper contains COM interface specific code. A COM wrapper usually need to reference to Microsoft PIA[5] to provide interface to Excel.

---

[5] PIA stands for Primary Interop Assembly. It provides interoperability programming interface between C# and Microsoft office products. We will need it in developing any Microsoft office related applications such as Excel UDF libraries.

To decide what code is put into which project depends on whether this code can be shared or is specific to one usage. For example, we should not put reference to *Office PIA* in the *AppLib* project because otherwise we will force all other clients implicitly have this Excel specific dependencies. Sometimes we may need some Excel related common functions that potentially can be shared. For example, we may need some code which takes input data from an Excel *Range* object and translates to a hard core data type and vice versa. In such case, we should put the code in a separate common library and make this library reference to the *AppLib*. As a result, if we later want to embed an Excel worksheet in our *WebApp* application, we can make the *WebApp* project reference to that Excel common library in order to utilize those common codes. The following figure shows possible inter-dependency among these projects.

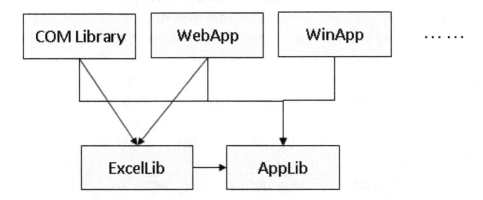

In practice, sometimes we may want to add a new delivery channel to an existing C# Windows application. For example, we may want to add an Excel user interface, an ASP.NET client, web service interface or wrap this application as a standard Windows service. If this existing Windows application solution has the above described solution structure, it will be relatively easy by simply adding one new client project into the solution. However if the original solution is a single project solution, we may have a problem. This is because we can only reference to a library project, not an executable project in C#. One solution to this problem is to make the existing project bigger by adding more code. However technically we cannot produce multiple executables from one project. Therefore we may have to make our executable smart enough to support different parameters and behave differently according to these parameters. Even if this approach works, we may end up with making our executable over complicated.

A more practical solution is to recompile the existing project as a C# library and then create a very thin Windows application project. This newly added Windows application project will contain just one Main class which contains one *Application.Run()* method to instantiate and launch the main *WinForm* of the original Windows application. It is easy to see that this overhead is very minimal. In return, we can now add different client projects to serve different purpose and make these projects reference to the recompiled library project.

The following figure shows the structure of this practical solution. The business logic part, including the *WinForms* part, is essentially the original Windows application that has been simply recompiled as a library. The *WinForms* box contains Windows application specific code. The rest is common business logic. Ideally we should separate them as shown in Figure 10 on page 109. But here we take a tactic approach in order to have a quick win.

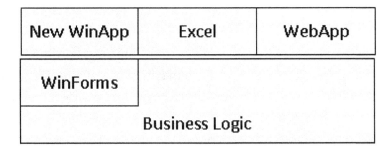

In the next several sections, we will discuss some popular types of client applications and their associated practical issues. Unless otherwise mentioned, we assume that logic layer is written in C#.

5.3   C# Application as Client Application

C# is an excellent technology to develop client desktop applications. Comparing with Visual Basic, C# is as easy to use but provides much more powerful features. It may be a reasonable predication that C# will gradually replace VB as the language of choice to develop rich Windows desktop applications.

This chapter is not going to discuss in detail how to develop desktop applications using C#. There are lots of computer books that are dedicating to this topic. Instead, we will only discuss some unique C# features that are very relevant in developing front office applications. This may be especially interesting to front office technologists who are coming from Visual Basic background.

Visual Basic does not expose multithreading interface to developers. But C# does. In fact, multithreading support is one of most important feature enhancements C# provides to developers over VB. Another related interesting feature that has been made possible by multithreading support is asynchronized callbacks. Using the callback technique can make desktop applications more efficient and flexible. For example, we can easily develop a market data monitoring program that listens to real-time market data at the background and update the screen when new data becomes available.

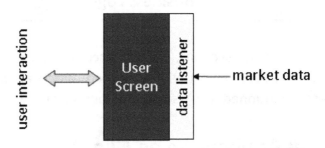

Figure 11 A Real-time Market Data Monitoring Application

A natural design for such an application is to make the data listener a callback running at the background. When new pieces of market data become available, the data listener will update the user screen. This design is very intuitive. However in order to make it work, we need to understand how multithreading should work in a GUI setup. This is somewhat a bit confusing.

The fundamental principle is that only the thread that creates a control can update that control. For example, let's assume that we have a textbox control on the user screen. Typically this control is created by the main thread that creates all the window forms and associated control components. The data listener callback is usually a separate thread that is driven by the arrival of market data. This means that the callback thread is usually not the same thread that has created the textbox control. Therefore, according to the principle we have stated at the beginning of this paragraph, the data listener callback cannot update the textbox control directly. As a result, the following code does not work:

```
/// <summary>
/// This method will be triggered by the Data Listener upon
/// receiving market data
/// </summary>
public void MyCallback(String data)
{
  myTextBox.Text = data;
}
```

Instead, we should program in the following way, i.e. passing a delegate to the control itself and let it decide when and how to update its contents. As shown in the code below, we associate the *DisplayMarketData*() method with a delegate. In the *MyCallback*() method, instead of calling *DisplayMarketData*() directly (which will violate the thread ownership rule), we will pass this delegate to *BeginInvoke*() method of the current window. As the current window is the owner of the textbox, by passing the delegate to it, we transfer the actual update task to that window therefore avoid violating the thread ownership rule.

```
/// <summary>
/// This method will be triggered by the Data Listener upon
/// receiving market data
/// </summary>
public void MyCallback(String data)
{
  // myTextBox is the textbox that will display the received
  // market data
  if (myTextBox.InvokeRequired)
```

```
  {
    BeginInvoke(myUpdateDelegate, data);
  }
  else
  {
    myUpdateDelegate(data);
  }
}

private delegate void UpdateDelegate(String data);
/// <summary>
/// Will be initialized with new UpdateDelegate(DisplyMarketData)
/// in the constructor
/// </summary>
private UpdateDelegate myUpdateDelegate;
/// <summary>
/// Updates the textbox with the realtime data
/// </summary>
public void DisplyMarketData(String data)
{
  myTextBox.Text = data;
}
```

Example 26 Update a Control from a Non-Owner Thread

5.4   VB Application as Client Application

Visual Basic is one of the most popular programming languages for desktop application development. There are far too many existing VB applications running on any trading floor. Even though C# (and sometimes Java) is gaining more and more ground, there are still many exiting VB applications that are not going to retire any time soon and, meanwhile, many new VB applications are being actively developed.

VB applications can work with C# programs nicely because both are COM compatible. To use a VB component in a C# program is very easy. All we need to do is to reference that particular VB component in our C# library. In fact, as we have explained in the previous book *C# in Front Office*, C# only knows the referenced component is a COM object and does not even realize it is written in VB.

From the other direction, i.e. using a C# component from a Visual Basic application requires a little more consideration. Firstly we need to make the C# component COM visible. This can be done easily by using the *ComVisble* attribute as we have used it in Chapter 1 of the previous book *C# in Front Office*. A skeleton of a COM visible class is shown below. We also need to mark the .NET assembly *ComVisible*. Such details have been discussed fully in the previous book and can also be found online at MSDN. Therefore we will not expand in detail here.

```
[ComVisible(true)]
[ClassInterface(ClassInterfaceType.AutoDual)]
[Guid("4130F708-C0FE-4c9c-9D37-B07B0472C586")]
public class MyComponent
{

}
```

After a C# component becomes a standard COM component, we can refer it in a VB project as usual. In fact, we have already seen a few such examples in previous book, for instance, when we were talking about how to use VBA to debug a C# RTD server.

However sometimes merely making a C# component COM visible is not enough. A commonly seen issue is related to multithreading. We know Visual Basic does not provide multithreading support to the developer but C# does. So if the C# component uses multithreading technique, we need to make sure it will not cause threading related issues on the VB component side. Taking Figure 11 on page 114 as an example, the main application may be an existing VB program and the data listener may be a newly added function implemented by a C# component. If we are listening to multiple real-time market data, the C# data listener will have to be multithreaded. This is because real-time market data may arrive simultaneously and independently from different sources. However if the client application is written in VB, the C# component cannot simply pass through all the data to VB side upon receiving them because otherwise it may cause thread related undesirable results. As a result, the C# component must deliver received data to the main VB application in a sequential manner.

There are many different techniques that can be used to serialize data delivery. One of the simplest and most intuitive techniques is to make the method that is responsible for delivering the data to the VB side a synchronized method. To do this, we can create a lock for that particular method so we can try to acquire that lock every time we enter this method. A sample code skeleton is shown below:

```
public void SendDataToVB(object data)
{
  // code that does not require serialization, e.g. preparation
  lock (myLockForSendDataToVB)
  {
    // code that require serialization
```

```
  }
  // code that does not require serialization, e.g. wrapup
}
private object myLockForSendDataToVB = new object();
```

In some cases, we can simply lock the entire method, i.e. something like the following:

```
public void SendDataToVB(object data)
{
  lock (myLockForSendDataToVB)
  {
    // code that require serialization
  }
}
private object myLockForSendDataToVB = new object();
```

In this case, C# offers a simplified syntax to make the method itself synchronized. A synchronized method means only one thread can execute this method at any time. (For people with Java background, it is equivalent to a synchronized method in Java.) The above code segment is equivalent to the following:

```
[MethodImpl(MethodImplOptions.Synchronized]
public void SendDataToVB(object data)
{
  // whatever code (please note we don't need lock any more)
}
```

Example 28 Interface with VB (using Synchronized)

No matter which approach we take, the objective is to serialize calls to VB side by ensuring only one thread at a time can execute the code that interfaces with VB. As a result, the code at C# side can be multithreaded, but the interaction with VB will be single threaded.

5.5 Excel as Client Application

Excel is ubiquitous on a typical trading floor. It will be very difficult to find a trading floor where you don't see Excel running on users' screen.

In a typical front office environment, quite often Excel is frequently used as a full featured application instead of a simple spreadsheet. To some extents, Excel is a great choice of developing user interface for front office applications. This is because many front office applications need to present lots of data to the users. Therefore the focus is how to display large amount of data in an organized and flexible way. In addition, a front office user will need to analyze data using his or her specific way or create some custom charts from these data. All of these are what Excel is good at. Thus it makes sense to use Excel as the user interface instead of re-inventing wheel to develop something similar. What is also important is that many front office users are skilled Excel users. Therefore using Excel as user interfaces means less user training which could be translated into better user satisfaction and higher productivity.

There are many different ways to use Excel as user interfaces. But all share more or less the same architecture. For example, both UDF and RTD technologies as discussed in the previous book *C# in Front Office* are good examples of using Excel as user interfaces. The core component is a C# library which produces various numbers and supplies them to an Excel spreadsheet for displaying to the users. Most examples given in these two topics so far are relatively simple and usually stateless[6]. In practice, sometimes such libraries can be more complex and even hybrid of UDF and RTD libraries.

When using Excel as user interfaces, we can also use Excel's built-in dependency support. If one cell is depending on other cells, this cell will be automatically re-evaluated if any of its depending cells' has changed. This is a very useful feature in developing many front office applications.

Let's continue using an interest rate yield curve library as an example. We know an interest rate curve is constructed using some market data as input. Therefore if any market data has changed, an interest rate curve will need to be reconstructed. In addition, there may be dependency relationships among different interest rate curves within a library. Therefore if one curve has changed, some other curves will need to be re-constructed too. As such, a practical question is how to ensure minimal reconstruction if one or more curves may need to be rebuilt. That is, if some market data or reference data have changed, we want to ensure that only those affected curves will be rebuilt but not those unaffected. This is very important to build an efficient real-time yield curve library.

For discussion purpose, let's assume we have a simple curve library which contains two curves. *Curve 1* is constructed from *Market Data Set 1*. *Curve 2* is constructed from *Market Data Set 2* and *Curve 1*. The following figure demonstrates the relationship among these objects.

---

[6]   Here, statelessness means no state information is maintained internally.

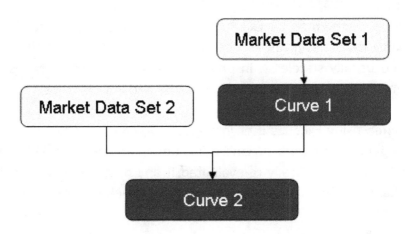

It is quite clear that if any element in *Market Data Set 1* has changed, both curves need to be re-constructed. But if any element in *Market Data Set 2* has changed and *Market Data Set 1* stays unchanged, only *Curve 2* needs to be rebuilt.

There are at least two approaches to establish these dependency relationships. One is to code them within the library itself. The other is to rely on Excel dependency check.

In the first approach, a typical design will have the following Excel UDF interface:

= BuildOrUpdateCurves(MarketData)

Here, *Market Data* is a combined set of both *Market Data Set 1* and *Market Data Set 2*. This approach basically is a black-box approach to the end users. This is because whether and how minimal rebuilding is implemented is up to the library developers completely. From the developers' perspective, the easiest approach is always to rebuild both curves regardless of which market data has changed. However this solution is clearly not efficient because of potential unnecessary rebuilding. To implement minimal reconstruction, developers must build a dependency tree (like the previous figure) inside the library. This is usually not an easy task in practice. A typical curve library may contain many different curves and large amount of different input data. What can make things more complex is that developers may need to improve and enhance such libraries on a continuous basis. This means that the internal dependency tree may keep changing accordingly because of new input data or new curve types. If the dependency tree breaks for whatever reasons, the consequence may be severe and even left unnoticed. This is because if any curve fails to be reconstructed when it should, users may be misled and/or use an obsolete curve without knowing it. This can mean big financial losses to the business.

The second approach is to modulate the curve library and delegate the dependency tree to Excel. In this approach, a typical Excel UDF interface design will have the following program interface:

```
Curve1 = BuildOrUpdateCurves1(MarketDataSet1)
Curve2 = BuildOrUpdateCurve2(MarektDaetSet2, Curve1)
```

Such interface is the most natural mapping of the dependency as shown in the previous figure. Each formula clearly describes which input data that the output depends on. Therefore it is up to Excel to determine whether and when a cell that contains such formula should to be re-evaluated. In another word, it's up to Excel to ensure minimal reconstruction. From this regard, this design is much cleaner and lighter than the previous one.

However in order to ensure minimal reconstruction work, there is an important detail we must make it right. This is how to make sure that re-constructing *Curve1* will trigger re-constructing *Curve2*.

While market data usually refers to one or more Excel ranges which contain the actual data feed, internal objects such as curves are usually represented as a handle to the users. A handle can be just a number or, more often, a string which is the name as the curve ID or name. For example the first formula may simply return a string such as *"Curve1"*. So the problem is after *Curve1* has been reconstructed, its handle may stay the same. This will prevent Excel from re-valuing the 2nd formula because Excel may mistakenly think all the inputs to the 2nd formula stay the same. This will cause reconstruction of *Curve2* to be mistakenly skipped. A simple but effective approach to address this problem is to append a version number after the handle. For example, instead of returning *"Curve1"*, the 1st formula can return something like *"Curve1:1"*. If the Curve1 is reconstructed, it will return *"Curve1:2"* to indicate it is a 2nd version of the same curve. This will force Excel to revalue the 2nd formula as one of the formula inputs has changed (i.e. from *Curve1:1* to *Curve1:2*). Internally, support of versioned handle names is easy to implement. This is because we can always extract the real handle name and its associated version number from a versioned handle as long as the encoding scheme is known. From that, we can continue using whatever algorithm that we use to process regular handle (i.e. without versioning number) by discarding the version number. Alternatively, if we wish, we can always implement a more advanced algorithm by also considering the version number. This can be very helpful if we need to allow multiple versions of the same curve to co-exist.

In reality, both approaches can work. But usually the 2nd approach is preferred due to the following reasons:

- It is easier for the users to see the relationship between inputs and outputs, i.e. which curve is built from which market data and which depending curves. In many cases, users want to know such relationships for their own benefits so that they can understand better and sometime troubleshooting themselves. Therefore users usually will be happier to know these relationships. This can be easily translated to better user satisfaction and higher productivity. Certainly this will help reduce unnecessary burdens on front office technologists too.
- It guarantees minimal reconstruction in a clean and reliable way without additional development efforts.
- It is easy to accommodate new requirements and changes with lower risk of messing up existing system. This is because we don't need to maintain the dependency tree, we will not have the chance to mess up the dependency and curve rebuilding logic.
- To some extents, the 2nd approach is a subset of the 1st approach. This is because the 2nd approach represents the logic of building all these curves regardless of implementations. Therefore the 1st approach will have to implement equivalent logic of the 2nd approach anyway. Essentially we can say that the 1st approach equals to the 2nd approach plus custom developed dependency tree logic.
- Following the previous point, if needed, we can always "upgrade" the 2nd approach to the 1st approach by adding some new code to handle dependency tree.

5.6 Web Client

Web interfaces have become more and more relevant in front office environments. This may not necessarily be because banks want to allow external customers to access some functions over internet. Sometime it is due to various technical and operational reasons. For example, banks may want to deploy web based thin clients to internal users instead of traditional desktop applications. This will help ease some practical system deployment issues such as system upgrade. Another example is web service. It is one of the standard and easiest solutions for cross platform integration. Banks have so many different systems that are built using different technologies and running on different platforms. Using web service is a cheap and quick solution to allow these systems to communicate with each other.

Developing web service or ASP.NET clients is relatively easy in C#. This is especially true if the overall system design follows the tiered architecture as shown in Figure 10 Tiered Architecture. For example, to expose a regular C# method as a web method, it may only require decorating the method with a *WebMethod* method attribute. This means all we need to do is to have a very thin interface class that contains a list of web methods we want to expose. Each of these web methods can be a one-to-one mapping with some methods that are available in the logic layer.

In practice, there is one thing we need to pay attention to regardless of whether the interface is web service or ASP.NET. We know that both web service and ASP.NET are HTTP based. Therefore both are synchronized which means a client sends a request and expects to receive the result via response. Therefore it may be a problem if the core logic is implemented using asychronized technologies such as callbacks for efficiency reason. For example, for some expensive operations (e.g. exotic derivative pricing etc), we may need to implement callback mechanism within the core logic library. This allows the client to send a request and walks way to perform other tasks while the expensive request is being served. When the result becomes available, a callback will be issued to notify the client with the result. This design will work great with other regular client applications (e.g. C# desktop application). It is especially handy because asynchronized callback is supported by C# natively. However callback is usually not possible with a web client. This is because asychronized call will not be blocked therefore the web client will get a null result. As such, we need to convert asynchronized callbacks to synchronized calls within the web client layer. This is quite similar to the case where the client is a VB client.

There are many techniques that can do this job. Let's assume that we have an asynchronized callback mechanism which has been implemented as following:

```
public interface ICallbackReceiver
{
   void Notify(object data);
}


public interface IJobServer
{
   void SubmitRequest(ICallbackReceiver requestor, object input);
}
```

Usually a client will implement the *ICallbackReceiver* interface. Then when this client needs to submit a request to the server, it can invoke the *SubmitRequest*() by passing *this* pointer and the input data. This *SubmitRequest*() method will return immediately so that the client can continue doing whatever it need to do without waiting for the request having been fulfilled. After this request has been fulfilled, the server will invoke the *Notify()* method to return the result.

Within this framework, one way to build a synchronized web interface is to do something similar to the following.

```
public object MyWebMethod(object input)
{
  MyConvertWorker myworker = new MyConvertWorker();
  myServer.SubmitRequest(myworker, input);
  object result = myworker.WaitForMyResult();
  return result;
}

prviate class MyConvertWorker: ICallbackReceiver
{
  public void  Notify(object data)
  {
    myResult = data;
    mySignal.Set();
  }
  public object WaitForMyResult()
  {
    mySignal.WaitOne();
    return myResult;
  }
  private AutoResetEvent mySignal = new AutoResetEvent(false);
  private object myResult;
}
private IJobServer myServer;
```

Example 29 Convert Asychronized Callback to Synchronized Call

The above code is reasonably self-explanatory. It introduces a helper class, *MyConvertWorker*, which acts as an intermediate between the *myWebMethod*() and the *myServer* (i.e. which actually fulfill the job request). What this helper class does is to block itself until the server notifies it with job results. This is done by a typical thread signaling mechanism which is similar to the one which has been described in Chapter 4 on page 51. It will block the current function until having received a response so that the original requestor will receive the result as if the function call is synchronized.

There is another subtle point in converting an asychronized callback to a synchronized call in the context of a web client which we sometime must pay attention to. It is HTTP request timeout. This setting is usually configurable on a web server. A typical default setting is between 10 and 30 minutes. This means if it takes too long for the server to complete a job, the request will timeout. Practically, even if we configure the timeout setting to a sufficiently long period, it may not be a good idea to keep a HTTP connection live (and idle) for such a long period. This is because it is clearly a waste of resource to keep an idle connection for an extended period and may also be prone to unexpected errors. Therefore in case that some jobs do require very long processing time, we may consider taking some alternative approaches. One approach is to break such function into three separate functions:

- SubmitJob(InputData) which returns a unique reference ID
- GetJobStatus(ReferenceID) which returns job status
- GetJobResult(ReferenceID) which returns actual job result

In this design, *SubmitJob*() will simply pass the job request to the real processing server. It will also generate a unique reference ID and associate it with this job request. This unique reference ID will then be returned to the web client immediately. This job ID will serve as a receipt for the web client to check job status and retrieve job result later.

From the web client's perspective, it can submit a job request and then walk away to perform other tasks. Periodically it can pull the job execution status by calling the *GetJobStatus()*. If the job has been completed, the web requester can then call the *GetJobResult()* to retrieve the result.

The similarity between this web based pulling model and the original callback model is that both are asynchronized. This means that the result will not be returned by the initial job submission function call. Instead, the result will be delivered to the client later. The difference between these two models is how a client gets the result. In the pulling model, the client needs to proactively pull the job result. But in the classical callback model, a client does not need to actively do anything special. It will be notified when the job result becomes available. As a result, in order to use the classic callback model, a client must support multithreading. But the pulling model can work with both single threaded and multithreaded client.

6 Debugging Tips

6.1 Display Custom Debug Information

Let's assume we have a *Security* class as defined below. It is pretty simple and nothing fancy at all.

```
class Security
{
  public String Exchange { get; set; }
  public String Ticker { get; set; }

  public Security(String exchange_, String ticker_)
  {
    Exchange = exchange_; Ticker = ticker_;
  }
}
```

In a debug session, we will see the following information as shown in the figure below. That is, we can only see information of the variable *me*'s class type, instead of its contents. In order to dig out the contents of the variable *me*, we need to expand the data or inspect the variable in a watch window.

```
class Program
{
    static void Main(string[] args)
    {
        Security me = new Security("NYSE", "MSFT");
                  ⊞ ◈ me  {DebugDisplaySample.Security}
        return;
    }
}
```

Figure 12 Display Default Debug Information

Clearly, in this example, we usually don't care about the data type of the variable *me*. Instead, we care about the contents of this variable because we are in a debug session. Therefore it will be much more convenient if we can see the contents of the variable *me* directly. This is shown in the figure below.

```
class Program
{
    static void Main(string[] args)
    {
        Security me = new Security("NYSE", "MSFT");
                  ⊞ ◈ me  "NYSE":"MSFT"
        return;
    }
}
```

Figure 13 Display Custom Debug Information

Such feature, i.e. displaying variable contents directly in a debug session, is automatically available for some built-in data types such as integer etc. So the question is how to enable this useful feature on other classes that are written by the developers?

There are several ways to achieve this goal. We will explain these different approaches one by one.

2.1.5. Method 1 – ToString()

The first method is simply to override the *ToString*() method. If we have the following *ToString*() method defined for the Security class, we will see Figure 13 above in a debug session.

```
public override string ToString()
{
  return String.Format("{0}:{1}", Exchange, Ticker);
}
```

In fact, displaying the result of *ToString*() method is the default behavior in a debug session. To see this, we can first comment out the above *ToString*() method i.e. do not override the *ToString*() method and then run the following code in a command window:

```
class Program
{
  static void Main(string[] args)
  {
    Security me = new Security("NYSE", "MSFT");
    Console.WriteLine(me.ToString());
    return;
  }
}
```

We will see the following output. This is the same as the information that we saw in Figure 12 on page 132.

```
DebugDisplaySample.Security
```

This method is very handy and ideal for those classes that we will override the *ToString*() method anyway. We can control exactly what we want to display in a debug session and the format we want to use. For example, in the example given above, we can have a ':' inserted between the stock exchange and ticker name.

However, this approach only works if we want to see exactly the same information in a debug session as the output of *ToString*(). Sometimes this may be inconvenient. For example, if we have a very complex class, we may need to have a *ToString*() method that will faithfully output all the fields. This will be too much information for a debug session. Instead, we only want to see some key data in a debug session. Let's imagine we have extended the above *Security* class to include other information such as company name, company description, industry, credit rating, current price and other related information. For the *ToString*() method, we want to display all these information. However in a debug session, we may still want to see stock exchange and ticker only. In this case, we can not achieve what we want using this approach.

2.1.6. Method 2 – DebuggerDisplay Attribute

Another approach is to use the *DebuggerDisplay* attribute. This will gives us with more flexibility than the previous approach that uses the *ToString*() method.

As an example, the following code will also produce the same information as shown in Figure 13 on page 132

```csharp
using System.Diagnostics;

[DebuggerDisplay("{Exchange}:{Ticker}")]
class Security
{
  public String Exchange { get; set; }
  public String Ticker { get; set; }

  public Security(String exchange_, String ticker_)
  {
    Exchange = exchange_; Ticker = ticker_;
  }
}
```

Figure 14 Using DebuggerDisplay Attribute

The code is pretty simple and self-explanatory. Before we move further to explain the usage of this *DebuggerDisplay* attribute, we need to point out that this attribute has higher priority than the *ToString()* method. This means if we have a class which has both the *DebuggerDisplay* attribute and an overridden *ToString()* method, we will see the information as defined by the *DebuggerDisplay* attribute in a debug session.

The simplest usage of the *DebuggerDisplay* attribute is to treat its contents as a format string where you can use {} to include a class member (variable, property or method). For example, in the sample given above, we use "{Exchange}:{Ticker}" which says to print the value of the member *Exchange* first, followed by a constant string ":" and finally the value of the member *Ticker*.

We can also invoke any method inside {} within this *DebuggerDisplay* attribute. Let's see the following example:

```csharp
[DebuggerDisplay("How about this: {ToString()}")]
class Security
{
  public String Exchange { get; set; }
  public String Ticker { get; set; }

  public Security(String exchange_, String ticker_)
  {
    Exchange = exchange_; Ticker = ticker_;
  }

  public override string ToString()
  {
    return String.Format("{0}:{1}", Exchange, Ticker);
  }
}
```

This code will produce the following result:

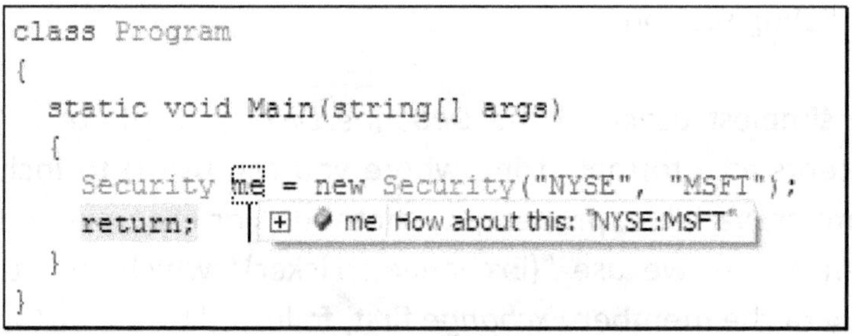

```csharp
class Program
{
  static void Main(string[] args)
  {
    Security me = new Security("NYSE", "MSFT");
    return;        ⊞ ⌀ me  How about this: "NYSE:MSFT"
  }
}
```

Figure 15 Display Custom Debug Information (calling method)

In addition, we can also use some simple expressions within this *DebuggerDisplay* attribute. For example, we can call methods on the member variable within {}. In the above example, we know *Ticker* is a *String*, therefore we can call the Length attribute on it.

```
[DebuggerDisplay("{Ticker.Length}")]
```

The above code will produce the following result:

```
class Program
{
    static void Main(string[] args)
    {
        Security me = new Security("NYSE", "MSFT");
        return;       ⊞  ♦ me  4
    }
}
```

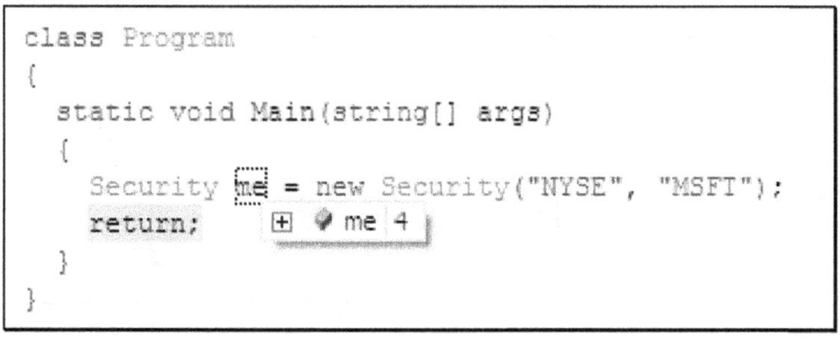

Figure 16 Display Custom Debug Information (calling attribute)

We can also apply some simple operations:

```
[DebuggerDisplay("{Ticker.Length + Exchange.Length * 3}")]
```

The above example will produce the following result:

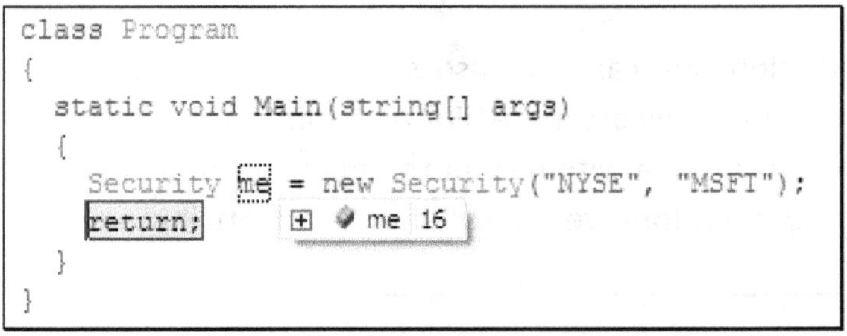

```
class Program
{
    static void Main(string[] args)
    {
        Security me = new Security("NYSE", "MSFT");
        return;          ⊞  ◆ me  16
    }
}
```

Figure 17 Display Custom Debug Information (applying operations)

The following is another slightly more complicated example:

```
[DebuggerDisplay("Ticker: {Ticker == null? \"NOT SET\" :
Ticker}")]
```

It will produce the following result:

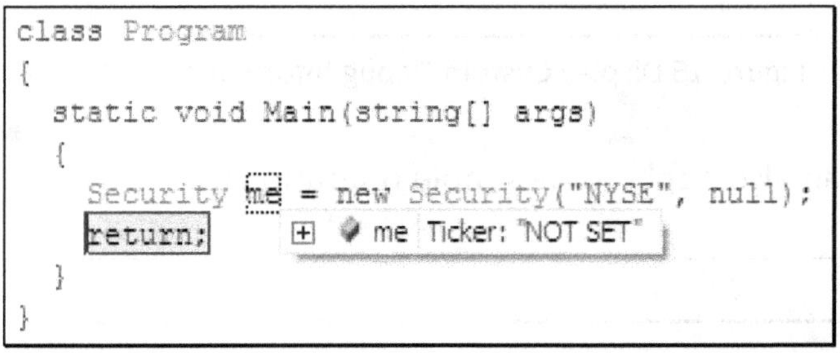

```
class Program
{
    static void Main(string[] args)
    {
        Security me = new Security("NYSE", null);
        return;          ⊞  ◆ me  Ticker: "NOT SET"
    }
}
```

As we can see, essentially the debugger will evaluate everything inside the {} as a C# expression. It will then concatenate those results with any remaining constant strings that are not enclosed with {}. The final result will be displayed in a debug session.

2.1.7. Method 3 – autoexp.cs

This method is in fact built upon the previous method. As we have already seen, the *DebuggerDisplay* attribute is powerful. However it is part of class source code. Therefore we need to modify the source code if we want to see different information in a debug session.

In addition, as this attribute is defined in the source code, all the developers will see exactly the same information in a debug session. In another word, it does not support user based customization. Sometimes this is inconvenient. For example, we may have a library that is developed by another team. Not all classes that are defined in that library have *DebuggerDisplay* attributes. This means that even if we have a debug built of that library, we still cannot see proper debug information that we want to see. However modifying source code of other team's work may be inappropriate. In other cases, we have full control of some libraries that we have developed ourselves. But different developers may want to see different information of a complex class that is suitable to their specific needs in debug sessions.

Therefore, ideally we want the debug information

- can be defined outside source code
- can be configured on a per-user basis

These are achievable and, surprising or not, very straight-forward. In order to do these, all we need is to customize a configuration file. This file is named as *autoexp.cs* and is located in the following directory *My Document\Visual Studio 2008\Visualizers*.
Below is a segment of the default *autoexp.cs* that comes with Visual

Studio installation. If we understand the usage of *DebuggerDisplay* as explained in the previous section, we can easily understand this file.

```
// System.Drawing
[assembly: DebuggerDisplay(@"\{Name = {fontFamily.Name}
Size={fontSize}}", Target = typeof(Font))]
[assembly: DebuggerDisplay(@"\{Name = {name}}", Target =
typeof(FontFamily))]
```

Figure 18 autoexp.cs

Each line of this file defines debug information for one data type. For example, the first line defines debug information that is associated with the *Font* type. We can see that it is easy to define debug information for our own classes by following these examples.

For example, the pervious debug information for *Security* class can be defined in the *autoexp.cs* file as following:

```
[assembly: DebuggerDisplay(@"\{Ticker = {Ticker},
Exchange={Exchange}}", Target = typeof(Security))]
```

Index of Examples

Example 1 Process Vectors and Matrices   12

Example 2 MyDateAdd   21

Example 3 Hide Unwanted Functions (A Simple Approach)   25

Example 4 Hide Unwanted Functions (A Better Approach)   27

Example 5 Debug-able Dynamic Script   36

Example 6 MyScriptUtil.StartDebug()   41

Example 7 A Debuggable User Script   41

Example 8 Compile Script in Debug Mode   42

Example 9 Dynamic Script Driver   44

Example 10 Lock Statement   55

Example 11 Interlocked class   57

Example 12 Monitor.Enter() / Monitor.Exit()   58

Example 13 Monitor.TryEnter()   60

Example 14 Thread Re-entry   61

Example 15 ReaderWriterLock   66

Example 16 Deadlock   69

Example 17 Double-Checking   74

Example 18 Eliminating Unnecessary Locking   77

Example 19 Double Buffer Design Code Skeleton   83

Example 20 Exchange Data Information with a Thread   86

Example 21 Thread Synchronization   88

Example 22 Thread Synchroniztion (more than 2 threads)   90

Example 23 Thread Synchronization (Two-Way)   94

Example 24 Inter-Process Synchronization: Named Mutex   100

Example 25 Recommended C# Solution Structure   110

Example 26 Update a Control from a Non-Owner Thread   116

Example 27 Interface with VB (using lock)   119

Example 28 Interface with VB (using Synchronized)   119

Example 29 Convert Asychronized Callback to Synchronized Call   128

Index of Figures

Figure 1 Implementing Business Calendar etc Using Extension Method   22

Figure 2 Hide Unwanted UDF functions (1)   26

Figure 3 Hide Unwanted UDF functions (2)   28

Figure 4 Debugging Hybrid Application (Project Settings)   49

Figure 5 Debugging Hybrid Application (Attach to Process)   50

Figure 6 Race Condition   54

Figure 7 Double Buffer Pattern Used in Curve Building   82

Figure 8 Monte Carlo   96

Figure 9 Monte Carlo - Mapping between Data and Thread   97

Figure 10 Tiered Architecture   109

Figure 11 A Real-time Market Data Monitoring Application   114

Figure 12 Display Default Debug Information   132

Figure 13 Display Custom Debug Information   132

Figure 14 Using DebuggerDisplay Attribute   135

Figure 15 Display Custom Debug Information (calling method)   136

Figure 16 Display Custom Debug Information (calling attribute)   137

Figure 17 Display Custom Debug Information (applying operations)   138

Figure 18 autoexp.cs   140

www.ingramcontent.com/pod-product-compliance
Lightning Source LLC
Chambersburg PA
CBHW071209050326
40689CB00011B/2289